The Concord
Sudbury
and
Assabet
Rivers

The Concord
Sudbury
and
Assabet
Rivers

A Guide
to Canoeing, Wildlife,
and History

Ron McAdow

Illustrated by
Gordon Morrison

Bliss Publishing Company, Inc.,
P.O. Box 920, Marlborough, Massachusetts 01752

First Edition published 1990. Second Edition 2000

05 04 03 02 01   9 8 7 6 5

Library of Congress Cataloging-in-Publication Data

McAdow, Ron, 1949-
   The Concord, Sudbury, and Assabet Rivers: a guide to canoeing, wildlife, and history / by Ron McAdow; illustrated by Gordon Morrison.

 Includes biographical references
1. Canoes and canoeing — Massachusetts — Concord River — Guide-books, 2. Canoes and canoeing — Massachusetts — Sudbury River — Guide-books, 3. Canoes and canoeing — Massachusetts — Assabet River — Guide-books, 4. Natural history — Massachusetts — Concord River Region — Guide-books, 5. Natural history — Massachusetts — Sudbury River Region — Guide-books, 6. Natural history — Massachusetts — Assabet River Region — Guide-books, 7. Concord River Region (Mass.) — Description and travel — Guide-books, 8. Sudbury River Region (Mass.) — Description and travel — Guide-books, 9. Assabet River Region (Mass.) — Description and travel — Guide-books. I. Title.
GV776.M42C666 1990
797.1'22'09744

                                              90-38
                                              CIP

ISBN 0-9625144-4-6

Graphic design by Christine Anderson
Cover illustration by Gordon Morrison ©
Cartography by Barbara Mackey and Judy Mack

PRINTED IN THE UNITED STATES OF AMERICA
Bliss Publishing Company, Inc.
P.O. Box 920, Marlborough, Massachusetts 01752

To Allen H. Morgan

*Allen's devotion to this river basin
awakened in me reverence
for the wildness near at hand
and brought words
to these pages.*

CONTENTS

Part Three: Wildlife

Plants

Animals

Birds

MAPS

Notes to the Second Edition

This second edition incorporates changes to canoe access points that have occurred since the guide was first published ten years ago. Several sites are no longer suitable for public use, conditions have changed at several others, and five new access points have been added, indicated by number/letter combinations. The text describes all of these changes, and the new access points have been added to the maps.

A 29-mile stretch of the Sudbury, Assabet, and Concord rivers became part of the federal Wild and Scenic Rivers system in April 1999, culminating a 12-year effort initiated in 1987 by Sudbury Valley Trustees founder and Executive Director Allen Morgan in conversation with then Representative Chet Atkins. Continuing advocacy by SVT and other organizations and agencies, plus strong leadership from Congressmen Atkins and Marty Meehan, led to congressional approval of federal protection that is consistent with strong protective measures already enacted by local and state governments.

Wild and Scenic designation protects the rivers from federally initiated, funded or permitted activities that would harm the resource values identified during a two-year study. Scenic, ecological, recreational, historic/archaeological, and literary values were all identified. Because Wild and Scenic rivers must be free flowing, without dams or impoundments, the designated area ends at the Route 3 bridge over the Concord River in Billerica and extends upstream on the Sudbury River to the Danforth Street bridge in Saxonville and on the Assabet to 1,000 feet below the Damonville Dam in Concord.

In accordance with the River Conservation Plan prepared by the study committee, a River Stewardship Council has been appointed to advise on issues affecting the rivers. Its members represent the eight towns along the Wild and Scenic segment (Billerica, Bedford, Carlisle, Concord, Lincoln, Sudbury, Wayland and Framingham), the National Park Service, U.S. Fish and Wildlife Service, the Organization for the Assabet River, and Sudbury Valley Trustees, plus two members appointed by the governor. The council will provide a permanent forum for cooperative action that will benefit the rivers and resolve issues that transcend town boundaries.

March 2000

Foreword

Concord, to most Americans, conjures up images of "the rude bridge" where the American Revolution was born. But to those of us who are nature-oriented, or who have a literary bent, Concord means Thoreau, Whitman, Hawthorne, and the Alcotts; a coterie that left its legacy in writing, a legacy that persists to this day.

However, we should not ignore those who came later, walking the same trails and canoeing the same placid waters of the Concord River and its tributaries — birdwatchers, botanists and biologists who have given us an unbroken record of observation and nature appreciation for more than a century.

Primarily because of two men, William Brewster and Ludlow Griscom, we have a more complete long-term record of avian trends and environmental changes in the Sudbury Valley than we have for any other region in the United States with the possible exception of the environs of Philadelphia, where both Wilson and Audubon once lived.

My own wanderings in the Concord area began nearly sixty years ago when I was working on my first *Field Guide*. I have many fond memories and flashbacks of rambles along the river and through Great Meadows, not only with Ludlow Griscom himself, but also with some of his disciples and proteges — Bill and Annette Cotrell, Dave Garrison, and Allen and Alice Morgan, to mention a few, as well as Paul and Susie Brooks, who canoed a lot, and Dick and Brownie Borden, who had a lovely home overlooking the marshes where they filmed waterfowl for their television shows. Allen Morgan was subsequently executive vice-president of Massachusetts Audubon Society for more than twenty years. But had it not been for Ludlow Griscom, who put it all down in his *Birds of Concord,* building on William Brewster's voluminous journals, much of this flow of avian history would have been lost, almost as though it had never happened.

Griscom, trained as a museum curator, can be credited with two pioneering breakthroughs. He bridged the gap between specimen-tray ornithology and modern field birding — between the shotgun and the binoculars. But he was more than just a "lister," as some of his peers tended to label him. Because of the vast field of experience at his command he was able to analyze trends, the ups and downs, and the where, when, and why of things. He had an intuitive understanding of population dynamics.

When James Fisher, my English colleague, and I made our grand tour in 1953, before writing *Wild America,* our very first stop after passing through U.S. Customs was Concord. James wrote:

> The trouble about visiting Concord on April 19 with amiable and intelligent Americans was that the rebels tried to tell me about the shot heard round the world on April 19, 1775. Concord's quiet colonial wooden houses glinted in the April sun through April trees. . .a house nearby even had a glass-framed bullet hole. . . .We crossed the rude bridge that arched the flood and found that, no doubt by careful arrangement with the management, a flag was (indeed) to April's breeze unfurled. In the bare trees along the river bank was a busy flock of rusty blackbirds. Making noises like rusty hinges creaking, they rustled through the upper branches of some American elms and poplars at the place where once embattled farmers stood and the American Revolution was born. . . .Were they on passage there on April 19, 1775?

In a footnote he refers to Ludlow Griscom:

> Perhaps not; it was an exceptionally hot and early season, and the migrants may have gone on. The apples were in bloom on April 19, 1775, and the soldiers marching to Concord were overcome by heat prostration.
>
> Ludlow Griscom, *The Birds of Concord,*
> *Cambridge, Mass., 1949*

This new, instructive, well-written book by Ron McAdow with its evocative illustrations by Gordon Morrison, captures the spirit of the Concord mystique. The Concord, Sudbury, and Assabet Rivers are rich in wildlife and have a cultural heritage treasured by those who live along their banks, and they are best visited by canoe. As Ron McAdow comments, the rivers have a hundred ways to sooth nerves jangled by the pushes and pulls of human pressures. Thoreau would have agreed.

Roger Tory Peterson
Old Lyme, Connecticut

Introduction

The quality of a journey depends not just upon *where* you go, but upon *how* you go and *why*. The most memorable travels occur when each of these elements has a strong resonance of its own and when all are in harmony.

If the "where" of your journey is the wilderness (even a backyard wilderness) and the "why" is investigating the curiosities of nature or traces of human history, then your own feet have few rivals as the preferred means of locomotion. They won't move you fast enough to turn the passing scene into a blur; they are relatively silent; they stop on command; they leave the hands free to wield binoculars, hand lens, camera, or net; and they allow the penetration of cat-briar tangles and sphagnum bogs with little apprehension of mechanical catastrophe.

In my view the human foot has only one serious challenger as transport of choice for outdoor explorers: the canoe. Like feet, the canoe is admirably slow and silent and will get you places other vehicles (including feet) fail to reach. True, it does not leave the hands entirely free and will not stop instantaneously, a combination of failings that has left me or my partner entangled in stream-bank shrubbery more often than I care to admit. (Those who canoe for exercise rather than adventure might say *I* was at fault in such instances for birdwatching when I should have been paddling, a hopelessly rational point of view.)

For these drawbacks, however, the canoe compensates with its own special virtues. It permits access to an alternate highway and trail system, one that tends to be less crowded than the earthen and macadam networks, especially in the over-appreciated suburban wilderness of eastern Massachusetts. It changes familiar stomping grounds into exotic waterways: places that one knows intimately from a streamside trail are revised, refreshed, magically transformed from the canoe view. It acts as a kind of mobile wildlife blind; a canoe seems to arouse curiosity before fear in most birds and mammals, unlike the invariably frightening human pedestrian. Dragonflies that dart out of camera range when approached from the shore, perch imperturbably on prow and paddle. Best of all are those moments, impossible to duplicate on land, when you sit, motionless yet progressing silently, all your senses absorbed in the perception of enveloping nature.

Allowing the superiority of wilderness as a destination, of exploration of natural and human history as a raison d'être and of the canoe as vehicle, the success of the journey rests finally with the resources of the traveler. These are by no means to be taken for granted. I once spent twelve hours travelling down a magnificent, forest-lined neotropical river in a rubber raft with a party of fellow Yankees, all of them "nice people." To my naive amazement most of my raft mates regarded the intervals between rapids as so much "down time" between thrills. The day was filled with marvels: the communal roar like distant thunder of troops of howler monkeys; a rainbow flotilla of a thousand butterflies "puddling" on a wet bar; a roost of boat-billed herons staring down at us with outsized nocturnal eyes; a spectral white hawk startled from its perch but holding fast to a writhing black-and-yellow snake; basilisk lizards dashing across the surface of glassy backwaters on their hind legs; a small Mayan temple recently excavated after a thousand years of disuse; a perfume shop of smells, sweet, pungent and musky carried out of the rain forest on the humid air; a fishing bat skimming for its prey at dusk; and of course the whitewater, which was thrilling indeed. To most of my companions the essence of the day for which they had paid was the roller coaster ride; the tropical wonders that appeared in astonishing diversity were just so much stage scenery. They listened patiently as the naturalist pointed out the first toucans to cross the gorge above us. But their tolerance for such nature chat diminished rapidly. They soon faced away from the forest, toward each other and began to talk amongst themselves; mostly about shopping. And of course the naturalist soon got the message and fell silent, though the wonders never ceased.

My moral, I guess, is that you can get as much or as little from an outdoor experience as you like, and that more is better. Enter Ron McAdow and his fine new guide to the natural and anthropological sights, sound, smells and textures of the Concord, Sudbury, and Assabet Rivers.

A guide may be many things. At the most mundane but essential level it may be a map in prose form: "Turn left just before Grist Mill Falls." Mr. McAdow supplies this skillfully in Part I, as well as providing a full range of maps at appropriate points throughout the text.

Another guide essential for any outdoor venture worthy of the name is the kind that identifies what you are seeing: A little bright-yellow bird with a Lone Ranger mask? Graceful black-and-enamel blue insects with two pairs of wings? Robust aquatic plants with fan-shaped leaves? The forbidding, heavily fenced structure on the left? Mr. McAdow wisely avoids trying to be comprehensive in this area, but rather identifies those organisms and objects that are most likely to catch our attention and then refers us to a selection of the best field guides to fill in the inevitable gaps. Gordon Morrison's accurate and decorative pen-and-ink drawings add at least a thousand words per species.

The *best* guide is one with a human expression, and this in my view is where Mr. McAdow shines brightest. In addition to pointing the way and satisfying our curiosity, he passes along the *experience* of the rivers: their history, both geologic and human, their moods, their diurnal and seasonal changes, their literature, even the many indignities they have suffered at our hands. The author does this not by exhortation, a great stylistic failing of many guide books: "Stand on the peak and admire the spectactular view!" — but by conversing with us at appropriate intervals about riverine matters that interest him. His interest tends to be contagious.

The proof of Mr. McAdow's success at this kind of guiding is that his book is a good read even if you are lying on the couch on a dreary November evening fifty miles from the places described. You can (probably should) read this guide with pleasure before and after, as well as during, your outing.

One last word for those who wouldn't set foot in a canoe for all the oil in Saudi Arabia: Ron McAdow's *The Concord, Sudbury and Assabet Rivers* is just as useful and enjoyable to riverside strollers as it is to the paddling community.

Christopher W. Leahy
Director of Conservation
Massachusetts Audubon Society

*This we know. The earth does not belong
to man; man belongs to the earth. This we
know. All things are connected like the
blood which unites one family. All things
are connected.*

*Whatever befalls the earth befalls the sons of
the earth. Man did not weave the web of life,
he is merely a strand in it. Whatever he does
to the web, he does to himself.*

Chief Seattle, 1854

Putting In

There is a fine moment during a canoe launch. The boat floats in readiness. The canoeist leans forward over the canoe, hands grasping the gunnels, one foot already aboard. As the trailing foot kicks gently from shore, weight shifts to the canoe, which bobs lightly and glides away from the bank. Gracefully, without crunch of feet or roar of motor, the canoeist enters the river.

Life teems in these rivers, in thousands of forms, dazzling our senses. Bird flight, bird color, and bird song fill the air. Dragonflies and damselflies, the electronic insects, fly like robots, showing off their brilliant metallic bodies. We hear the hush of wind and buzz of wings, and the murmur of water rubbing stone. We feel the tug of a fish, or feast our eyes on the exorbitant scarlet of the cardinal flower. The rivers have a hundred ways to soothe nerves jangled by the pushes and pulls of our own species.

The Concord, Sudbury, and Assabet offer the canoeist calm flatwater paddles. . .but they also offer challenges depending on where you go and when you go there. One gentle outing begins with a launch into the Concord River from the Old Calf Pasture, at Lowell Road in Concord. From there it is a short paddle to Egg Rock where Emerson and Thoreau relaxed and reflected. Continue into the mouth of the Assabet, to fish for bass or crappie, or to watch kingfishers fly by, or perhaps, at a lucky moment, to see one plunge below the surface.

At sunset on a hazy summer night the meadows along the Concord River offer a fortune in light and air and bird-life. The lazy green water drifts along, bound north for the Merrimack, in no hurry, falling less than a foot in a mile. It barely has the power to keep vegetation from its channel. It hasn't the energy to ripple its own surface. The pale green marsh plants stretch to a distant woods. The big sky is peppered with birds. Young night herons lounge and socialize before they go to work, "quawk" being their sole remark, carrying all the meaning herons need.

Those who know how to handle a canoe in rapids can begin a lively Assabet trip at the Ben Smith Dam in Maynard, if there's plenty of water in the river. They can shoot through Maynard quickly, dodging the genuine hazards of fast-flowing water. After a short portage around the Powdermill Dam in Acton, quickwater continues through West Concord, where there's a tricky shoot of a broken mill dam. The river slows only at the end, to join sister Sudbury at Egg Rock.

The upper Sudbury is far from serene. The river's a rascal in Westborough, Hopkinton, Southborough, and Ashland. A broken mill dam lies deep in the woods, the fifth mill down from the headwaters. It's not easy to reach because shallow water and deep vegetation bar passage from above and below. When you find it, it's as though you've stumbled on a Mayan temple. Water tumbles through a breach in the old stone dam, cascading to the bed below. The portage must be improvised through a boulder-strewn jungle. Hikers prefer the ridge-tops to these soggy bottoms, for good reason. The footing is terrible. You can travel much farther to find less adventure than you can have on the upper Sudbury.

Whether we canoe to see birds, to fish, to explore, or to gaze at natural colors in natural light, our motive is the same. It is our craving for connection with the great flow of nature that takes us onto the water. The river itself has a kind of life. Its energy and matter tumble unsteadily through time and space, as do the energy and matter of an organism, hurrying, resting, and eddying by turns. Our little boats carry us into this metaphor, and while inside we are with muskrat and mink, heron and frog, hemlock and cattail. The abundant life of our valley concentrates along its rivers, and the rivers are best visited by canoe.

My hope is that you will use this book to share in the pleasurable learning that came my way while researching and writing it. The Concord Basin is rich in wildlife, rich in its cultural heritage, and rich in a citizenry that cherishes that heritage and that wildlife, and is willing to spend time and treasure to interpret and preserve them.

Key to River Maps

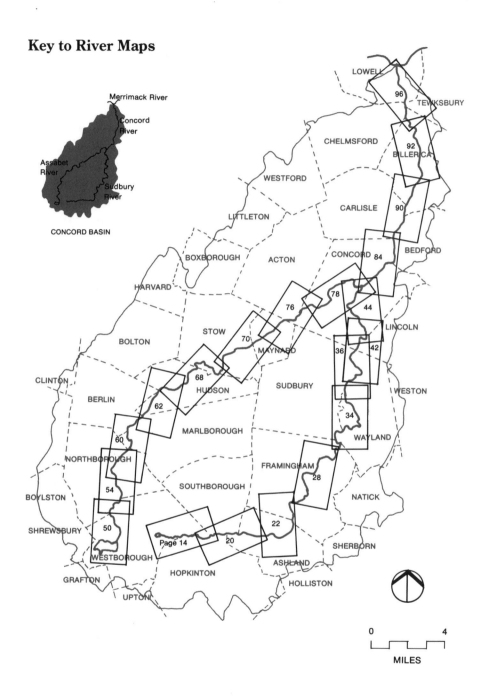

Merrimack River

Concord River

Assabet River

Sudbury River

CONCORD BASIN

LOWELL

TEWKSBURY

96

CHELMSFORD

92

BILLERICA

WESTFORD

CARLISLE

90

LITTLETON

CONCORD 84

BEDFORD

BOXBOROUGH

ACTON

HARVARD

78

STOW

76

44

LINCOLN

BOLTON

70

MAYNARD

36

42

68

HUDSON

SUDBURY

WESTON

CLINTON

BERLIN

62

34

60

MARLBOROUGH

WAYLAND

NORTHBOROUGH

54

FRAMINGHAM

28

BOYLSTON

SOUTHBOROUGH

NATICK

50

SHREWSBURY

Page 14

20

22

SHERBORN

WESTBOROUGH

HOPKINTON

ASHLAND

GRAFTON

HOLLISTON

UPTON

0   4

MILES

Part One: Canoeist's Guide

How to Use This Guide

Canoeists who do not know where they would like to paddle might start with the Suggested Outings Directory on page 199 in the Appendix. To plan a canoe trip on a given stretch of river, examine the map of that segment. The trip will begin and end with an access point, which is a place where canoes can be put into the water and cars can be parked. Access points are shown with a dot and labelled with a bold-faced number and name, which refer to the description in the text.

The contour maps are portions of composite USGS (United States Geological Survey) 7.5 minute topographic quadrangles. These useful maps are available in color from sources listed in the Appendix on page 202. The reproductions used here are slightly reduced, to a scale consistent throughout.

River-mile System

The purpose of the river-mile system is to name the locations of points along the rivers. It is intended to clarify the relative positions of the places mentioned, and to help canoeists predict how much time will be needed to reach a given destination. Distances are given from upstream to downstream.

Sudbury River is abbreviated as SU. Its starting point is the mouth of Cedar Swamp Pond in Westborough. Pantry Brook (SU mile 25.1) means that this tributary stream enters the Sudbury 25.1 miles downstream from the beginning of the river.

Assabet River is abbreviated as AS. Its starting point is the Nichols Dam in Westborough. Boundary Street (AS mile 7.6) means that Boundary Street crosses the Assabet River 7.6 miles below the Nichols Dam.

Concord River is abbreviated as CO. Its starting point is

at Egg Rock in Concord. Ball's Hill (CO mile 2.2) means that this hill is passed 2.2 miles below Egg Rock. The Concord River ends in Lowell, where it flows into the Merrimack River.

Right and Left

Right and left are generally used in preference to compass directions to indicate which side of the river something is on. Because the rivers wander in all different directions, orientation to the direction of flow is more useful to the canoeist. Right and left always refer to someone facing downstream.

Travel Time

How long it takes to cover a given stretch of river depends on the speed of the current, the wind, the strength of the paddlers, how often and long they stop, and, most of all, on portages, if there are any. In general, you can fish or birdwatch your way at about one mile per hour (mph). Steadier nonathletic paddling covers about two mph. Strong paddling down a good current zips along at five mph, and racers go much faster than that.

Information About River Sections

Four kinds of information are provided for each river section:

— map
— list of access points
— comments
— suggested outings

The comments cover the river from the most upstream point of access, then follow the river downstream to the end of the section. This arrangement of comments does not necessarily correspond to the suggested outings. Frequent reference to landmarks using the river-mile system is intended to guide canoeists to pertinent comments.

International River Classification System

Experienced canoeists are familiar with the American Whitewater Affiliation's International River Classification system. This system rates the difficulty of rapids so that canoeists may judge whether their training and equipment match what they will need on a given reach of river.

The canoeable portion of the Concord River is almost all flat water, as is the lower Sudbury. The difficulties posed for canoeists by the Assabet and the upper Sudbury fall into the Class I category, with the exception of the Class II run through Maynard. Class I water is described as having easy bends, small rapids with low waves, and obstacles like fallen trees and bridge pilings. The speed of the current is less than hard back-paddling speed.

In Class II water, a medium level of hazard is encountered: fairly frequent but unobstructed rapids with regular waves and low ledges. The river speed occasionally exceeds hard back-paddling speed. Class II rapids such as the stretch in Maynard should not be canoed without training in white-water skills.

A Note of Caution
The Sudbury Valley Trustees and the author are proud to offer this guide as a tool in planning canoe outings in the Concord River Basin. We emphasize that the information presented here to aid canoeists does not replace reliance on good sense and mature judgment. Canoeing is an adventure because of the unexpected circumstances, welcome or unwelcome, that are as unique to a moment in time as the weather. A newly windfallen tree complicates a downstream passage. Low water can force wading beside the canoe. High water creates hazards by increasing the river's energy. New property owners may deny access where previous owners permitted it. Availability of parking is subject to change. Those who enjoy the outdoors should adhere to the basic ethical standard of consideration for others and for our shared environment. Above all, responsibility for personal safety rests with each canoeist.

Canoe Equipment

If you canoe once or twice a year, you will probably rent or borrow the boat. If canoeing becomes an important recreation for you, you will want to buy a canoe. Here is a summary of points that must be considered in purchasing canoes and paddles.

Canoes
Materials
The most practical river canoes of our time are made of plastic laminates, sold under a variety of trade names.

The best of these materials combines lightness of weight, slipperiness and springiness on rocks, and high resistance to splitting and tearing.

Fiberglass is next best. It is less slippery and flexible, but easier to repair and less expensive.

Aluminum is not springy, it catches on rocks, and is noisy. It conducts heat too well; it feels cold when in cold water. It wouldn't make sense to take aluminum onto the rocky upper Sudbury or Assabet. On the deep water of the Concord and the lower Sudbury, the main drawback of aluminum is noise from bumping paddle shafts, lapping water, and brushing vegetation. For many, this will be considered a minor drawback when set against the durability of this material.

There are beautiful wooden canoes. Wood is quietest of all, but, due to its fragility, suited only for deep water.

Bullet-proof vests and expensive canoes are made of a high-tech fabric named Kevlar. Its light weight, flexibility, and strength make it a logical canoe material.

Wood-and-canvas was the mass production standard until about 1950. A wooden frame with many ribs was covered with canvas and waterproofed with paint. Wood-and-canvas requires maintenance. Although practicality argues for the newer materials, there's something appealing about all those ribs. Wood-and-canvas joins birch bark as a sentimental favorite of craftspeople and their admirers.

Size and Shape
The most difficult thing about buying a canoe is predicting the circumstances in which you will most frequently use it. Will you be on moving water, where current is the major consideration, or on open, still water, where wind is the problem? Will you and your partners prefer speed or stability? Will you paddle alone, or with others? Do you plan canoe camping trips in which the boat will be carrying heavy gear as well as people?

No canoe is ideal for all needs. If you can afford only one canoe, project its most frequent uses, and compromise.

Stability is achieved at the expense of speed. Narrow canoes with round bottoms go faster but feel tippier. (They are not necessarily easier to capsize.) Wide, flat-bottoms give stability, draw less water, and handle more easily in flowing water because they catch less current.

Longer canoes draw less water than shorter ones, are more easily propelled, hold course more steadily, and are more stable. They have more "shoot" after the stroke. Shorter canoes are easier to turn and fit better on small cars. The upper Sudbury and the Assabet have tight bends in which shortness is a virtue. An average canoe is seventeen feet long and weighs seventy-five to eighty pounds. The range of lengths is eleven to twenty feet. Canoes under sixty pounds may be considered light in weight; the range is thirty-three to over a hundred pounds.

Greater depth (higher sides) allows more freeboard, which is how much of the side is above the waterline. Deeper canoes ship less water from waves but are pushed more by wind. Upswept ends look nice but catch side winds.

A canoe has "rocker" if its keel profile curves up from the center toward each end. Rocker allows rapid pivots, good for maneuvering in rapids. Rocker catches wind on flatwater, and makes it harder to go straight.

On lakes (or on wide, slow rivers!) a keel along the bottom of the canoe helps it hold its course, reducing slide slip from wind. But keels retard sideways motion when it is desirable, as when negotiating rapids. Keels tend to catch on rocks. The shoe-keel is a flattened compromise.

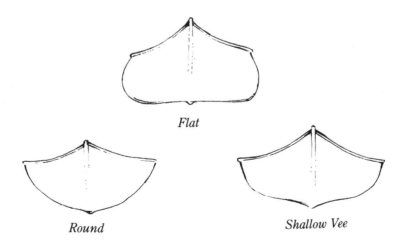

Flat

Round

Shallow Vee

Paddles

Materials

Handsome wooden paddles are made from spruce, maple, basswood, or ash. Spruce is light but less durable than the hardwoods; maple is strong and limber but is the heaviest; ash and basswood are in between. Composite (laminated) wooden paddles are strong and can have good springiness. Wood looks great and feels fine in the hands, after the varnish has been removed from the grips, which are thereafter preserved with applications of boiled linseed oil.

No wooden paddle can stand much jabbing into gravel or slamming into rocks, which is why plastic or aluminum-and-plastic paddles are better for shallow water. Since every canoe needs an extra paddle, buying one of each material is not extravagant.

Width

Experts argue about blade width. The range is six to eight inches. Wider paddle blades deliver more power per stroke but tire the paddler sooner. Indians paddled with narrow blades and quick strokes.

Length

The usual rule for proper paddle length is that when the blade rests on the toes, the paddle should reach to the chin. Like all rules of thumb, this one will bow to individual experience and preference. Stern paddlers often use longer paddles because they must reach farther to the side, and because they do most of the steering. Some canoeists like to stand up and paddle, and therefore use a six-footer.

Other Equipment

Casual paddlers need only personal flotation devices (life jackets), paddles, and a boat. But for journeys of exploration you should take additional supplies and equipment.

> First-aid kit
> Drinking water — more than you think you'll need
> Insect repellent
> Sunscreen
> Spare paddle
> Folding saw for removing small windfalls
> Rain clothes
> Hat
> Bandana

This guide and/or topographic maps
Sunglasses

For a trip that combines birding, photography, and fishing, the kit should include:

Binoculars
Field guide to birds
Camera in waterproof plastic box or bag
Ultra-light spinning rod and reel with a small spinner

Such spinners have brought in crappie, bass, bluegill, pumpkinseed, shiners, trout, chain pickerel, northern pike, and yellow perch; all in the Concord, Sudbury, and Assabet. Fish from the Sudbury below Ashland should not be eaten as they may be contaminated with mercury.

Clothing

Soft soles are preferable to hard, in a canoe. Old sneakers are good for wading. Wool socks have insulating value even when they're wet. Short pants don't protect you from poison ivy, thorns, mosquitoes, or the sun. Polarized sunglasses improve your vision into the water. Hats have too many virtues to list.

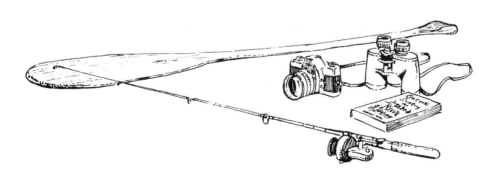

Safety

Canoeing in fast-moving water can be compared to alpine
skiing. In each case gravity hauls the sportsperson down
a slippery surface. The velocity depends on the gradient.
Immovable obstacles must be avoided. Failure to avoid
them can have serious results.

Safety depends, in each case, on maintaining control,
which means staying away from gradients that are too
steep for your ability, or courses that have many sharp
turns. In rivers, higher water in effect makes the slope
steeper by increasing the energy of the flow. High water
reduces obstacles below, but increases those overhead,
such as the undersides of bridges.

The notion that you have to paddle faster than the
current to steer the canoe is a dangerous myth. The
"steerage way" concept applies to boats that steer with a
rudder. Paddlers have several ways of handling their
little boats, the least of which is ruddering. When
approaching a challenging spot, back-paddling to slow the
canoe gives more time for "reading the water," more time
for communication between the paddlers, and more time
to position the canoe.

Training in canoeing is available from several
organizations listed in Appendix 2.

Weather

If an electrical storm catches you on the water, be aware
of the danger from wind and lightning. Paddle to shore
and take cover. If you are far from autos or buildings, find
a group of trees of approximately uniform height. Avoid
especially tall trees, trees in the open, and hilltops.

When preparing for a canoe trip, it is wise to assume
that you will find yourself in the water. Hypothermia can
be a danger if the water is cold. Do canoe in the colder
months, but think ahead to what you would do if you
became wet. Getting warm again shouldn't be too difficult
in this populous river basin. The danger lies in underes-
timating the threat of hypothermia.

Safe canoeing depends on sound judgment. Think
ahead to worst-case situations. Limit the risks, and limit
the degree of possible damage.

The Sudbury River

Thy voice is sweet, Musketaquid,
and repeats the music of the rain...
but the stream I love, flows
in thy water, and flows through rocks
and through the air and through the
rays of light as well, and through darkness,
and through men and women. I hear and see
the inundation and eternal spending
of the stream in winter and in summer
in men and animals, in passion and thought.
Happy are they who can hear it.

Ralph Waldo Emerson
Journal, 1856

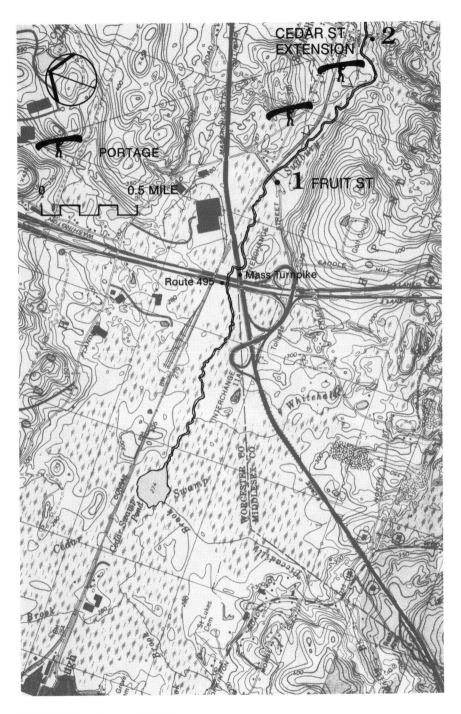

CEDAR ST EXTENSION

●.2

PORTAGE

0   0.5 MILE

●1 FRUIT ST

Route 495 ●   ● Mass Turnpike

USGS 7.5': Marlborough, Milford

Sudbury River: Towns of Hopkinton, Southborough, Westborough

Canoeing the Sudbury

Hopkinton, Westborough

Access Points

1 FRUIT STREET, Hopkinton (SU mile 1.7)
USGS Marlborough quadrangle
An unmarked gravel lane is off Fruit Street next to the
Southborough Rod and Gun Club. There is easy access
and parking where the lane reaches the river, just
upstream from the old bridge abutments.

2 CEDAR STREET EXTENSION, Hopkinton-
Southborough (SU mile 2.7)
USGS Marlborough quadrangle
Best access is on the right bank, above the bridge. On-road
parking is on the south side of the river.

Comments

The trip to Cedar Swamp Pond is not to be undertaken
lightly. The river has trouble finding its way out of
Cedar Swamp. Free-flowing water diminishes, amid
summer vegetation, to a scanty minimum. The upstream
passage is arduous, the return trip not much easier. The
payoff is the seldom-visited pond, source of the Sudbury. Unpeopled, unlittered, Cedar Swamp Pond boasts
a wealth of birds and wildflowers.

At the point of access, red maples shade the river. In
late summer, scarlet cardinal flowers will be seen here.
They prefer partial shade. So does sweet pepperbush
whose sweet aroma fills the late summer air.

Upstream from Fruit Street, the canoeist soon
emerges from the shade and enters a light-filled marsh.

15

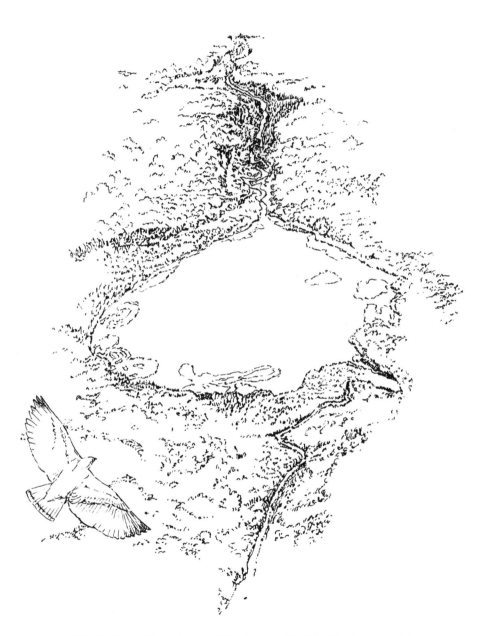

The Sudbury River rises in Cedar Swamp Pond in Westborough. It is seen here from the west, looking downstream.

The river, through the marsh, has tightly folded meanders not represented on the USGS topographical map.
The mileage noted above was measured on such a map.
If an odometer could be placed on a canoe, it would give
a higher figure. In bends such as these, a short canoe is
an advantage.

A concrete tunnel carries the river under the
Massachusetts Turnpike (SU mile 1.3), and then beneath
Interstate 495 (SU mile 1.2).

As the noisy highways are left behind, the great calm
of the swamp descends. The width of open water varies
from several feet to several inches; generally there are
about two feet of river between opposing smartweed
shoals. In most places the channel, though narrow, is
deep.

Frequently the channel is bordered with a woody
shrub called buttonbush, which blooms in late summer.
Each one-inch flower cluster is a white explosion of
spherical symmetry.

Whitehall Brook (SU mile 0.3) drains Whitehall Reservoir and western Hopkinton.

With perseverance, the unspoiled pond is reached at
last. The point of discharge into the stream is considered
the head of the Sudbury River. The pond, dark with
natural tannin, is bordered by yellow pond lilies and
swamp loosestrife, less gaudy than its purple cousin.
Swamp loosestrife is an agent of change. It turns pond
into marsh. Ponds are temporary; their vegetation even-
tually fills them up.

Eat lunch in the duck blind, reservations not required.
Or visit the quaking bog on the north edge of the pond,
but walk lightly; bogs are fragile. Metropolitan District
Commission borings taken in 1895 indicated that here the
peat moss was forty feet deep.

Some of the remaining Atlantic white cedars, after
which the swamp is named, stand to the south of the
pond. Others are to the north of the railroad.

There ought to be fine fish in this inaccessible pond.
My experiments failed to prove the hypothesis. Otters
have frequented the pond in the winter, but their pre-
dations are thought to help the game fish. Because otters
eat mostly the slower-moving, smaller fish, there should
be more food for the larger, faster individuals.

The downstream journey is less arduous. Dragonflies

and damselflies patrol territories of open water. Painted turtles scramble from their perches. Big snappers drowse in the muck.

The following birds were seen on an August outing: green-backed heron, gray catbird, eastern kingbird, mallard, wood duck, American goldfinch, swamp sparrow, common grackle, great blue heron, Canada goose, black-capped chickadee, and rose-breasted grosbeak.

This trip is easier in the springtime, in high water, before the vegetation grows back. Even then it is not a quick trip. But this big swamp and its little pond are worth some effort to see.

Suggested Outing
To and from Cedar Swamp Pond
Distance: 3.4 miles round trip
Portages: None
Parking: Off Fruit Street, Hopkinton, Access 1

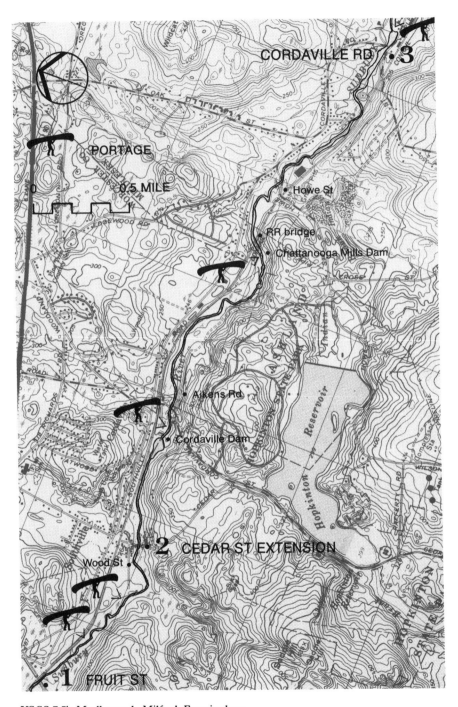

CORDAVILLE RD • 3

PORTAGE

0.5 MILE

• Howe St

• RR bridge

• Chattanooga Mills Dam

• Aikens Rd

• Cordaville Dam

Reservoir

Hopkinton

• 2 CEDAR ST EXTENSION

Wood St •

• 1 FRUIT ST

USGS 7.5': Marlborough, Milford, Framingham

Sudbury River: Towns of Ashland, Hopkinton, Southborough, Westborough

Canoeing the Sudbury

Hopkinton, Southborough, Ashland

Access Points

1 FRUIT STREET, Hopkinton (SU mile 1.7)
USGS Marlborough quadrangle
An unmarked gravel lane is off Fruit Street next to the
Southborough Rod and Gun Club. There is easy access
and parking where the lane reaches the river, just
upstream from the old bridge abutments.

2 CEDAR STREET EXTENSION, Hopkinton-
Southborough (SU mile 2.7)
USGS Marlborough quadrangle
Best access is on the right bank, above the bridge. On-road
parking is on the south side of the river.

3 CORDAVILLE ROAD, Ashland (SU mile 5.7)
USGS Framingham quadrangle
Access is from a boat ramp on the right bank, just
upstream from the bridge, on High Street. There is
parking for several cars.

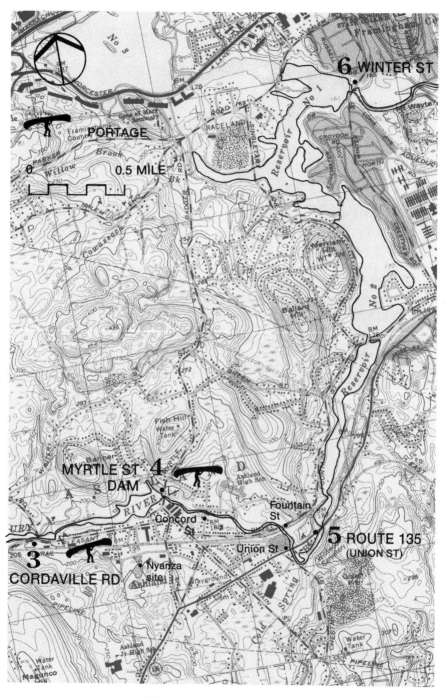

6 WINTER ST

PORTAGE

0   0.5 MILE

MYRTLE ST 4
DAM

3
CORDAVILLE RD

Fountain
St

5 ROUTE 135
(UNION ST)

Union St

Nyanza
site

USGS 7.5': Framingham, Holliston

Sudbury River: Towns of Ashland, Framingham

4 MYRTLE STREET DAM, Ashland (SU mile 6.5)
USGS Framingham quadrangle
It is easy to reach the pond above the dam; downstream
access is more difficult. Follow the trail along the left bank,
and cut through the trees to where the two strands of river
merge. Three or four cars may be parked near the dam.

5 ROUTE 135/UNION STREET, Second bridge, Ashland
(SU mile 7.5)
USGS Framingham quadrangle
On the left (west) side of the bridge, a driveway leads to a
commercial parking lot alongside the river.

6 WINTER STREET, Framingham (SU mile 10.3)
USGS Framingham quadrangle
A chain link fence with a pedestrian gate narrows access
to the left bank of the river. Parking on nearby side streets
is difficult; it's best to be dropped off. A shallow gravel bar
and swift current make this a tricky launch.

Comments
The *River Guide* published by the Appalachian Mountain
Club describes the Sudbury River above Saxonville (north
east Framingham) as "impractical for canoeing." With the
exception of the two short trips described below, the upper
Sudbury *is* impractical. It is narrow and frequently obstructed. It offers many surprises, some welcome, some
not.

Just below the put-in at Fruit Street, the sites of the
uppermost of the Sudbury's mills are reached. The 1831
map labels these as "Morse's Mills." At the first, the
ancient headrace diverts some water to the left, but canoeists should keep to the main channel, which goes to the
right. Not far below is a dam that must be portaged. Take
out on the right, carry fifty yards along the road, and
bushwhack back to the river.

From here the Sudbury River is the boundary between
Southborough, on the left, and Hopkinton, on the right.
Passage is blocked by many small fallen trees. Some of
these may be stepped over, as the canoe passes beneath.
At other points wading will be necessary while the canoe is
see-sawed over a log. The river disappears into the roots
and under the trunk of a large deadfall, necessitating a
portage of one hundred yards along the railroad to the left.
Stay alert. There are many trains.

The Wood Street Dam (SU mile 2.4) is at one of the prettiest places on the river. The dam has been breached, but the rapids require portaging. The portage is on a path to the left. The property owners have been sympathetic with considerate canoeists. Be careful carrying across the millrace. Put in on the pool below the rapids.

Much bedrock is exposed in this area, and there are many large boulders. The rock is an attractive pink biotite granite, named for the biotite mica that gives the rock its dark speckles. This granite is similar to the extensively quarried Milford granite found a few miles to the south.

The Sudbury flows quietly between big boulders, past red maple swamp. Look for cardinal flowers in August. The Cedar Street bridge (SU mile 2.7) is just below the back yards of Wood Street.

Below Cedar Street Extension, the railroad tracks run alongside on the left. To the right are woods and marsh. Mink and even river otters have been seen along this stretch. It's an excellent place to see wood ducks. The water is deep, the current manageable, and the trout fishing is good in spring and early summer. This idyll ends at Cordaville, where the dam (SU mile 3.3) creates a shallow pond. The portage is three-tenths of a mile. Take out to the left of

This dam provided water power and jobs at a village called Chattanooga, on the Sudbury River in Ashland. The dam is now broken, and the village reclaimed by forest.

the dam and carry along the right side of the chain link fence, to the driveway for the construction company parking lot. Carry along the driveway to Route 85 (River Street, Southborough). Cross the highway and the river to Aikens Road. A very short distance down that road, the river may be entered from its right bank.

Downstream from Route 85 (SU mile 3.5) the river offers the canoeist pretty scenery and one headache after another, in the form of shallows, deadfalls, boulders, and vegetation in the channel. Those who persevere will be carried into a lost corner of Ashland. At SU mile 4.3 stands a large dam, breached and overgrown. This was once the center of a thriving mill village called Chattanooga.

The first use of waterpower at this site was a forge built by Andrew Newton in 1745. It is said to have made cannons for Washington's army. In 1846, the year that this part of Framingham combined with pieces of Holliston and Hopkinton to become Ashland, a paper mill went into operation here. The Chattanooga Woolen Mills succeeded the paper mill. In 1879 it had 75 employees operating 42 looms. The mill burned in 1890. One by one, the other structures also burned. Now the site of the entire village is a haunted, peaceful place in the forest.

The difficulties of reaching Chattanooga are nothing compared to those of getting around its dam. It must be portaged on the right. Carry along the dam. There is a considerable drop on its downstream side. Bushwhack through the marsh and boulders back to the river. Beware of the lush growth of poison ivy.

A short distance below Chattanooga the river passes under the railroad tracks. It continues narrow, marshy, shallow, and troublesome. A nice trout pool is just below Ashland's Howe Street (SU mile 4.8). Fallen trees, informal dams, shallow water — and glorious, immediate nature — continue to confront the canoeist. Informal dams are rows of casually placed stones which create an obstruction in low or moderate water levels.

Cordaville Road (SU mile 5.7) has good access on the right above the bridge. Below the bridge and across a pond is a small dam, skirted on the right by an easy portage. The river flows quickly for a stretch, then eases into the impoundment formed by the dam at Myrtle Street. Pollutants from the Nyanza toxic-waste site enter the Sudbury here, seeping through the soil of the right bank. (See page 116.) From here on, Sudbury River fish are considered inedible, as indicated by signs. The dam at Myrtle Street (SU mile 6.4) is portaged on the left. A low, informal dam may require a see-saw portage a short distance below. Beyond the Concord Street bridge (SU mile 6.7) the river runs behind houses, passes through a narrow, overgrown area, and reaches Fountain Street (SU mile 7.1) and Route 135 (SU mile 7.2). Just past Route 135 (Union Street), Cold Spring Brook enters from the right, carrying the outflow from the reservoir at Ashland State Park. At the mouth of Cold Spring Brook is a water intake. Through this intake, Ashland Sand and Gravel Company formerly removed Sudbury River water, used it to wash sand, and returned the water to the brook at a point upstream.

The Metropolitan District Commission Reservoir #2 begins where the river goes under Route 135 (SU mile 7.5) for the second time. Boating is not permitted on the reservoir. The takeout is on the left, at a parking lot just before the bridge.

Suggested Outings
— Cedar Street (Hopkinton-Southborough) Up to the pool below the Wood Street rapids. Down to the mill pond at Cordaville. Return to start.
Distance: 1.8 miles round trip
Portages: None
Parking: On Cedar Street Extension, Access 2

— Cordaville Road (Ashland) Upstream past Howe Street. Return to start.
Distance: 2.2 miles round trip
Portages: None, but numerous fallen trees. Some sections may require wading.
Parking: Between river and High Street, Access 3

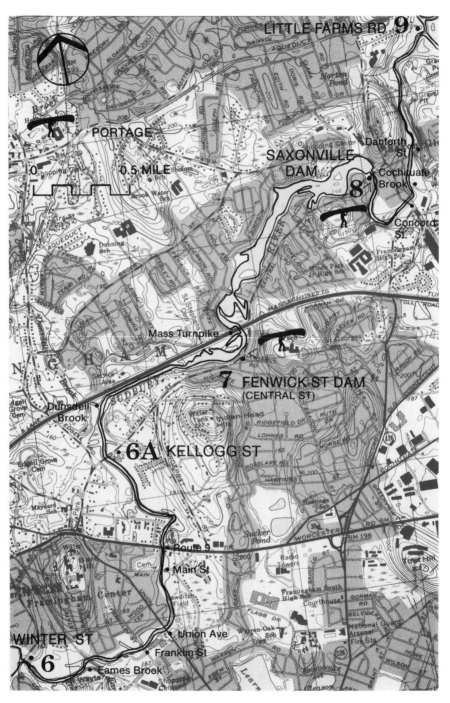

USGS 7.5': Framingham

Sudbury River: Town of Framingham

Canoeing the Sudbury

Framingham

Access Points

6 WINTER STREET, Framingham (SU mile 10.3)
USGS Framingham quadrangle
A chain link fence with a pedestrian gate narrows access
to the left bank of the river. Parking on nearby side streets
is difficult; it's best to be dropped off. A shallow gravel bar
and swift current make this a tricky launch.

6A KELLOGG STREET, Framingham (SU mile 12.0)
USGS Framingham quadrangle
A new access off Kellogg Street is on the right bank of the
river upstream from the Central Street bridge. An unpaved
driveway leads into parking area and launch site.

7 FENWICK STREET DAM/SIMPSON PARK, Central
Street, Framingham (SU mile 13.1)
USGS Framingham quadrangle
This low dam causes the only portage between Winter
Street and Saxonville. There is easy access on either side
of the dam, above and below. Park on Haynes Street and
cross Central Street with caution.

8 CENTENNIAL PARK/SAXONVILLE DAM, Framingham
(SU mile 14.6)
USGS Framingham quadrangle
Take out well above the dam at a small park indicated by a
Sudbury Valley Trustees sign on the right bank of the river
at the dead-end of Centennial Place.
Below the dam, a path leads down to the right bank of the
river from a street light next to the bridge. There is park-
ing for several cars on Centennial Place.

9 LITTLE FARMS ROAD, Framingham (SU mile 16.1)
USGS Framingham quadrangle
This dead-end street, off Elm Street, provides ideal river
access. The parking area is owned by the Framingham
Conservation Commission. There is a turn-around, parking
for at least eight cars, and two good places to put canoes on
the river.

Comments

Through eastern Ashland and western Framingham, the Sudbury's former channel is flooded beneath reservoirs owned by the Metropolitan District Commission. At Winter Street, the Sudbury ends its career as a lake and becomes a river once again. It flows through densely populated Framingham, between banks that have been straightened to "improve" nearby real estate.

At Winter Street, access is on the left bank, near the mouth of Baiting Brook. That brook and its tributaries drain the northwest corner of Framingham, which is the most rural section of town. Ten minutes of paddling gains the first landmark, Eames Brook, and a railroad bridge (SU mile 10.7). The large brick building on the right is the Framingham incinerator building. Franklin Street is just downstream. Below its bridge, the right bank becomes a steel wall.

In a pinch, the downstream embankment of Union Avenue (SU mile 11.2) could be used for access. The next bridge, "Old Main Street," is out of service.

Route 9 (SU mile 11.7) is supported by tremendous I-beams, rather low over the river, which may not admit canoe passage when the river is flooded. It has been suggested, without much hope, that a drawbridge be installed on Route 9 for the benefit of canoeists. The generous width of the channel under the bridge prevents the low clearance from causing difficulty except during floods.

Where the Sudbury winds to the north of Framingham Center, a small farm occupies the left bank. Two goats and a donkey sometimes greet those paddling by. Central Street crosses at SU mile 12.2. Dunsdell Brook and the Massachusetts Turnpike are encountered at SU mile 12.4, both on the left. The current, which has thus far been steady, diminishes. The Sudbury is confined to a long, straight, wide ditch to the south of the Turnpike. The signs announcing Exit 13 are visible, but useless to the canoeist. This is the only part of the trip for which automobile transport might be preferable.

The Fenwick Street Dam (SU mile 13.1) is only three feet high, but several drownings have resulted from people being too casual about its hazards. The dam is easily portaged on either side. The river can be conveniently entered here, as suggested below for the second outing, to picnic at Framingham conservation property on the left bank, 0.6 miles downstream, facing the wooded island.

After passing under the Massachusetts Turnpike (SU mile 13.4) the river broadens into a lake bordered with lily pads. The banks are back yards of this residential area. The Saxonville Dam (SU mile 14.6) is the last dam on the Sudbury. It was built on the site of the falls where, in springtimes past, Indians gathered to fish. The mill building stands on the river's left bank, bearing a large "Roxbury Carpet Company" sign, naming the last in a series of companies that made carpets and carpet yarns here beginning in 1837.

The bedrock below the dam appears jet black, but unweathered exposures beneath the bridge show that it is greyish green. It is a chlorite schist called prasinite. The color is from a soft variety of the mineral mica, of which it is largely composed.

At Saxonville Falls native peoples gathered in the spring to obtain ocean fish that migrated up the Sudbury River to spawn.

To continue downstream, portage the Saxonville Dam on the right. Cross Central Street and go to the street light next to the bridge. From there, a path descends to the right bank of the river. The water is fast here, and sweeps alongside the mill wall at the left. This creates a spiralling current that tends to push the boat against the wall. Dexterous effort is needed to avoid bumping the wall and rocks in the channel. Framingham North High School is beyond the right bank.

The current remains rapid under Concord Street (SU mile 15.3) but slows at the mouth of the Cochituate Brook (SU mile 15.4), the outflow from Lake Cochituate. Goldfish sixteen inches long have been spotted under the Russian olive tree at this junction.

The Danforth Street bridge (SU mile 15.6) marks the halfway point in the length of the Sudbury River. Though only halfway horizontally, vertically the Sudbury is almost home. It has done nearly all of its falling.

The next half-mile of the river is idyllic. The steep, wooded banks embrace the river and calm the canoeist. This is a fitting preamble for canoeing the rest of the river, because it continues serene.

Little Farms Road (SU mile 16.1) and the upstream entrance to the oxbow are on opposite sides of the river. The end of the road is on the left. The mouth of the oxbow is on the right. The eastward-sweeping oxbow is a mile-long detour in the river's natural channel. In 1957, a cut was made across the base of the oxbow. The former channel still has some water, and even a little current. If there is enough water, you can paddle into the upstream end of the oxbow. A causeway is reached one-fifth of a mile into the oxbow. This was built to give a gravel company access to the interior of the oxbow. A narrow passage through the causeway has been re-opened. It is possible to work your way through the narrow passage, to continue to Pod Meadow, and, circling counter-clockwise, to come to the downstream end of the oxbow not far below where you entered.

Henry David Thoreau stopped here on a rowboat journey in July, 1859. He paced off the width of the oxbow neck: one hundred yards.

The Little Farms Road access is near both mouths of the oxbow.

Suggested Outings
— Across Framingham
Distance: 4.3 miles
Portages: 1 short carry
Parking:
    Upstream: Winter Street, Access 6
    Downstream: Saxonville Dam, Access 8

— Picnic at Simpson Drive Conservation Area
Distance: 1.2 miles round trip
Portages: None
Parking: Fenwick Street Dam, Access 7

— From Little Farms Road, upstream to the mouth of
Cochituate Brook. Return to upper entrance to the oxbow.
Explore the oxbow.
Distance: Variable
Portages: None
Parking: Little Farms Road, Access 9

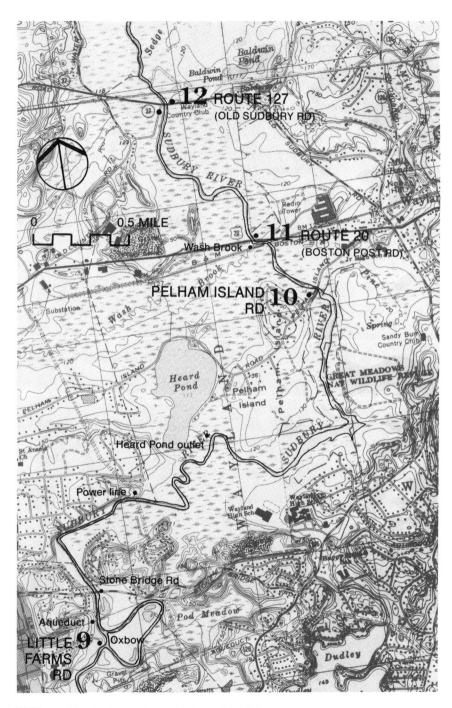

USGS 7.5': Framingham, Concord, Maynard, Natick

Sudbury River: Towns of Framingham, Sudbury, Wayland

Canoeing the Sudbury

Framingham Sudbury, Wayland

Access Points

9 LITTLE FARMS ROAD, Framingham (SU mile 16.1)
USGS Framingham quadrangle
This dead-end street, off Elm Street, provides ideal river access. The parking area is owned by the Framingham Conservation Commission. There is a turn-around, parking for at least eight cars, and two good places to put canoes on the river.

10 PELHAM ISLAND ROAD, Wayland (SU mile 19.8)
USGS Natick quadrangle
The left bank of the river below the bridge offers good access. Roadside parking accommodates five or six cars.

11 ROUTE 20 (Boston Post Road), Wayland (SU 20.3)
USGS Framingham quadrangle
On the right side of the river, just below the bridge, access is provided by a dirt and gravel boat ramp. Seven cars can be parked on the fringes of the area.

12 ROUTE 27 (Old Sudbury Road), Wayland (SU mile 21.3)
USGS Framingham and Maynard quadrangles
Just upstream from Route 27, River Road runs along the left bank for a few hundred yards. A boat ramp gives easy access. Cars can be parked along the road.
A second point of access at the end of a spur road (Old Route 27) near the entrance to the Wayland Country Club, is no longer accessible by car. The River Road access is preferable.

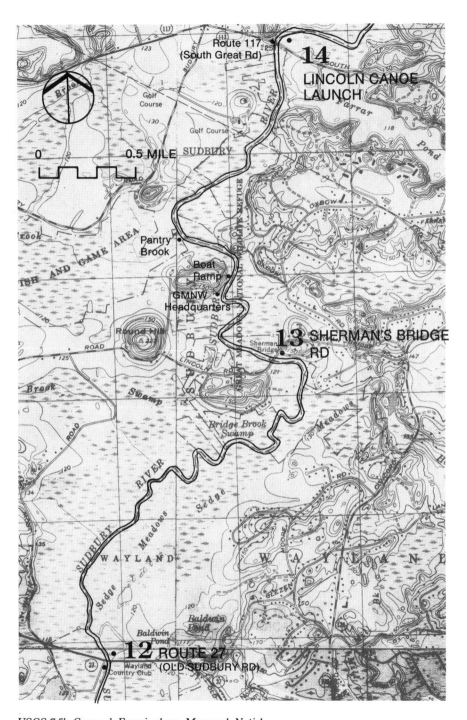

USGS 7.5': *Concord, Framingham, Maynard, Natick*

Sudbury River: Towns of Concord, Lincoln, Sudbury, Wayland

12 ROUTE 27 (Old Sudbury Road), Wayland (SU mile 21.3)
USGS Framingham and Maynard quadrangles
Just upstream from Route 27, River Road runs along the
left bank for a few hundred yards. A boat ramp gives easy
access. Cars can be parked along the road.
A second point of access at the end of a spur road (Old
Route 27) near the entrance to the Wayland Country
Club is no longer accessible by car. The River Road access
is preferable.

13 SHERMAN'S BRIDGE ROAD, Wayland (SU mile 24.0)
USGS Concord quadrangle
This access point has boat ramps on the right bank, above
and below the bridge. Parking for six or seven cars is in
pulloffs adjacent to the boat ramps.

14 LINCOLN CANOE LAUNCH, Route 117 (South Great
Road), Lincoln (SU mile 26.5)
USGS Concord quadrangle
One-tenth of a mile below Lee's Bridge, on the right, a
slough has been dredged to a canoe landing site. Parking
for ten cars is fifty yards up the trail. Signs and the
parking lot are visible from Route 117, in a grove of pines
200 yards east of Lee's Bridge.

*Stone Bridge joined Wayland and Sudbury for nearly a century before one span
washed out during a flood in 1955.*

37

Comments

Downstream from the Little Farms Road access, the lower entrance to the oxbow appears on the right. When there's enough water to float the canoe, venture in. The center of the oxbow is now a swampy, wooded, uninhabited island. One-half mile upstream a large marsh, called Pod Meadow, stretches to the east. The combination of habitats produces many bird species and magnificent bird song in the springtime.

The aqueduct from Wachusett Reservoir (SU mile 16.2) passes overhead in the form of a huge steel pipe. More water passes through that pipe than passes under it in the same time.

Stone Bridge Road (SU mile 16.3) crosses on a newish bridge. The name refers to the original land owner, not a building material. Just beyond is the striking, truncated, stone bridge that once linked the village of Wayland to its parent town, Sudbury. The west span washed out during the Hurricane Diane flood in 1955. This venerable structure has become a visual emblem of the heritage of the Sudbury Valley. The sixty cannon General Knox brought from Fort Ticonderoga to force the end of the siege of Boston were hauled across the Sudbury River at this point, over an earlier bridge.

The sharp right bend at SU mile 16.7 occurs at the corner of a well-defined L-shaped glacial deposit that bounds this southeast corner of Sudbury. Such a steep bank, appearing to be all of sand and none of bedrock, is an example of an ice contact deposit. The embankment formed during the glacial period when sand piled high against the side of a block of ice.

Major power lines cross at SU mile 17.2, beyond which the river opens up into the Broad Meadows, which stretch on the right bank toward the grounds of Wayland High School. These meadows gave the river its Indian name, Musketaquid, the river where grass grows.

The Sudbury meanders toward Heard Pond. The outlet from the pond (SU mile 18.1) is not always well defined. In high water, the passage braids between marshy islands. Carp spawn in the shallows here. The pond and adjacent woods are prime birding zones. The woods to the north of the pond were purchased by Sudbury Valley Trustees and transferred to Great Meadows National Wildlife Refuge. Wayland has preserved the former Erwin Farm, to the east of the pond, as the Heard Farm Conservation Area. In the first outing suggested below, the Heard Pond area is explored before the return to Little Farms Road.

Pelham Island Road skirts the north shore of Heard Pond, with convenient canoe access if the pond and its immediate environs are the sole object of your visit.

A broad marsh is on the opposite side of the river from Heard Pond. In previous decades, marsh wrens nested in the cattails here.

Below Heard Pond, the river is fringed with a woody shrub called buttonbush, which recurs in patches all along the Sudbury. Buttonbush is adapted to withstand flooding.

At SU mile 18.9 the river turns sharply to the left. An outcropping of stone is visible on the right, a metamorphosed granodiorite, much older than the granite of the upper Sudbury. A trail leads up from the river to fields and woods at Greenways Conservation Area, owned by Sudbury Valley Trustees and the Town of Wayland. A canoe landing here provides access to Greenways' trails. Sunfish nests may be visible in the shallow water below the embankment. These shallow depressions in the sand, six inches in diameter, are built by bluegills and pumpkinseeds, both members of the sunfish family.

Sandy Burr Country Club appears on the right bank farther along.

To the left below Pelham Island Road (SU mile 19.8) is the marsh drained by Wash Brook, which is a nest area for marsh wrens. Tributaries include Sudbury's Hop Brook. A railroad bridge and the Route 20 bridge (SU mile 20.3) are near each other; Wash Brook enters the river between them, through a culvert under the railroad embankment.

The easy access at Route 20 makes this stretch tempting for casual outings. Below the bridge, the Sedge Meadows spread on both sides. The inside of the first meander supports a large shoal of submerged plants: elodea, pondweed, fanwort, coontail, and watermilfoil. By midsummer wild rice raises its unique silhouette along these banks.

Red-orange posts mark the invisible passage of a Tenneco high-pressure gas pipeline, just above the River Road-Route 27 access (SU mile 21.3). Below the bridge, the old Route 27 roadbed, now closed to cars, no longer offers a good point of access on the right side. A historical marker stands where this road meets the Wayland Country Club, marking the location of a fight during King Philip's War.

The meadows reach their widest point below Route 27. Small maple trees dot the left bank at fifty-yard intervals below the bridge. The dark green floating plants with fan shaped leaves are water chestnut, an introduced Asian species which forms dense carpets along the bank during the summer.

Bridge Brook (SU mile 22.9) enters from the left through the swamp of the same name, but can't be seen except at high water. To the right is the former Watertown Dairy, now preserved as Sedge Meadows. A hill obstructs the direct northward passage of the river, so it meanders good-naturedly to the east, reaching Sherman's Bridge Road (SU mile 24.0) on the far side of the hill.

Suggested Outings
— To Heard Pond from Little Farms Road. This is a fine bird outing. Heard Pond is rich in wildlife, including fish. To navigate the channel between pond and river, moderate or high water is required.
Distance: 5 miles round trip
Portages: None
Parking: Little Farms Road, Access 9

— Downstream run of this section.
Distance: 7.9 miles
Portages: None
Parking:
    Upstream — Little Farms Road, Access 9
    Downstream — Sherman's Bridge Road, Wayland, Access 13

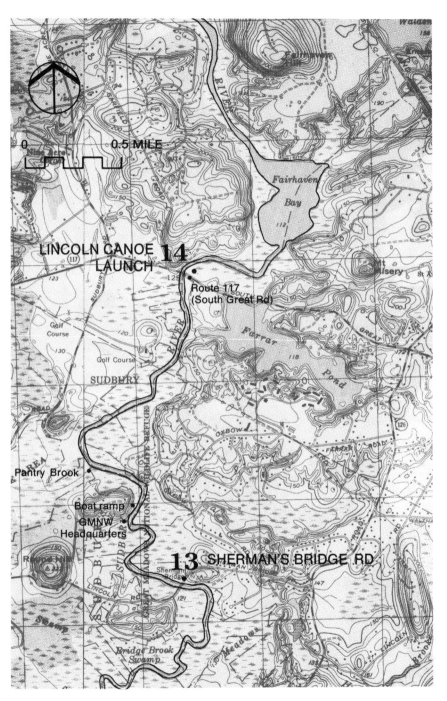

USGS 7.5': Concord, Maynard

Sudbury River: Towns of Concord, Lincoln, Sudbury, Wayland

Canoeing the Sudbury

Wayland, Sudbury, Lincoln, Concord

Access Points

13 SHERMAN'S BRIDGE ROAD, Wayland (SU mile 24.0)
USGS Concord quadrangle
This access point has boat ramps on the right bank, above
and below the bridge. Parking for six or seven cars is in
pulloffs adjacent to the boat ramps.

14 LINCOLN CANOE LAUNCH, Route 117
(South Great Road), Lincoln (SU mile 26.5)
USGS Concord quadrangle
One-tenth of a mile below Lee's Bridge, on the right, a
slough has been dredged to a canoe landing site. Parking
for ten cars is fifty yards up the trail. Signs and the parking lot are visible from Route 117, in a grove of pines 200
yards east of Lee's Bridge.

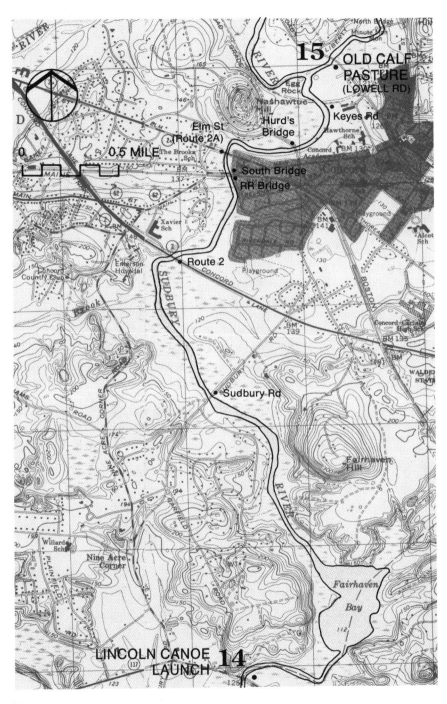

15

OLD CALF PASTURE
(LOWELL RD)

North Bridge
Minute Man Mon

Egg Rock

Nashawtuc Hill

Hurd's Bridge

Keyes Rd

Elm St
(Route 2A)

The Brooks Sch

Hawthorne Sch

Concord Acad

0   0.5 MILE

South Bridge

RR Bridge

Xavier Sch

Emerson Hospital

Route 2

Playground

Concord Country Club

SUDBURY

Sudbury Rd

Fairhaven Hill

Nine Acre Corner

Willard Sch

LINCOLN CANOE
LAUNCH

14

Fairhaven

Bay

USGS 7.5': Concord, Maynard

Sudbury River: Towns of Concord, Lincoln

14 LINCOLN CANOE LAUNCH, Route 117 (South Great
Road), Lincoln (SU mile 26.5)
USGS Concord quadrangle
One-tenth of a mile below Lee's Bridge, on the right, a
slough has been dredged to a canoe landing site. Parking
for ten cars is fifty yards up the trail. Signs and the
parking lot are visible from Route 117, in a grove of pines
200 yards east of Lee's Bridge.

15 OLD CALF PASTURE. Lowell Road, Concord
(SU mile 31.2; CO mile 0.1; AS mile 31.9)
USGS Concord quadrangle
A boat ramp and parking for about six cars are provided
at the Old Calf Pasture Conservation Area, which is on
the right bank of the river, just upstream from Lowell
Road.

Comments

Sherman's Bridge is wooden, with wooden railings, a relic
of a historic style. Below the bridge, two hills are visible
to the left. Round Hill, a reservation of the Sudbury
Valley Trustees, is the more southerly and more distant of
the two. The other, Weir Hill, comes right down to the
river. The headquarters building of Great Meadows
National Wildlife Refuge nestles on the eastern side of
Weir Hill. Boaters are encouraged to stop in for a visit.
Look for a concrete boat ramp (SU mile 24.8) on the left
bank. From the ramp it is a short walk back along the
river to this building, which contains educational exhibits
and literature about the refuge and its wildlife.

The mouth of Pantry Brook (SU mile 25.1) appears on
the left. In high water an ascent is possible into the area
owned by Massachusetts Division of Fisheries and Wild
life.

The meadows along this part of the Sudbury River, now protected as part of Great Meadows National Wildlife Refuge, are called the Broad Meadows. The view toward Wayland from the river justifies this appellation.

At Boundary Rock (SU mile 25.9) the boundaries of four towns form an X. Concord lies ahead to the left. Lincoln is ahead on the right. Wayland is behind on the right, and Sudbury behind to the left.

Lee's Bridge (SU mile 26.4) is a span of granite and concrete, connecting Lincoln to Concord via Route 117. Beyond the bridge, to the left, is an exposure of much-weathered granodiorite.

The Lincoln Canoe Launch is on the right, not far beyond Lee's Bridge. With its off-road parking and its proximity to Thoreau's famous haunts, this access point is deservedly popular.

Ospreys are sometimes spotted in this area.

Fairhaven Bay's western shore has a steep bank, rising to the ridge called Conantum. Fairhaven Hill lies to the north of the bay. The north bank of Fairhaven Bay has a stone boathouse. To its right is a marsh called Well Meadow. Walden Pond is less than a mile to the northeast, beyond Well Meadow. Much of the river bank is owned by the Concord Land Trust and the Lincoln Conservation Commission.

The grasses of Broad Meadows drew settlers to Sudbury and Wayland in 1639.

Yellow perch, bullhead, bluegill, pickerel, pumpkinseed, bass, and crappie are caught in Fairhaven Bay. By regional usage, bluegill and pumpkinseed are subspecies of the kivver. Thoreau called them bream.

Just downstream on the left an outcropping of the rock serpentinite forms "Martha's Point," which Thoreau called Bittern Cliff. Fairhaven Hill is opposite. On a late summer evening, cedar waxwings were seen flying out over the river here, plucking insects from the air. They hovered briefly, swooped and returned to their perches, piping their high-pitched calls.

The width of the river fluctuates from fifty to one hundred yards. The vegetation along the bank is buttonbush, in some places. Elsewhere are pond and water lilies with purple loosestrife at their rear.

Although it's easy to land a canoe below the Sudbury Road Bridge (SU mile 28.7), there's no safe place to stop an automobile.

Emerson Hospital comes into view below Sudbury Road. This stretch of the river holds a good population of vigorous bass and kivver. The river narrows gradually, and the current increases just enough to free its surface of duckweed and watermeal.

The Route 2 bridge (SU mile 29.5) is a single span of arching stone. Thoreau referred to the embankment on the left as "Clam Shell Bluff."

Residential Concord is on the right bank. A railroad bridge and South Bridge (SU mile 30.1) are upstream of Southbridge Boat House, where canoes may be purchased and rented. There is a fee for launching your own canoe from this location.

Elm Street/Route 2A (SU mile 30.2) has a triple arched bridge. Nashawtuc Road crosses Hurd's Bridge (SU mile 20.7). Neither of these offers practical access to the river. The left bank is marshy. The right bank consists of lawns, first of homes, then, past Nashawtuc Road, of Concord Academy.

The Sudbury makes its final leftward bend to face Egg Rock, then bends right to join the Assabet. In 1885, as part of the celebration marking the 250th anniversary of the founding of Concord, several tablets were set up marking places of importance. At this time, Egg Rock was inscribed:

On the Hill Nashawtuck
At the Meeting of the Rivers
And along the Banks
Lived the Indian owners of
Musketaquid
Before the White Man came.

On the right is a conservation area called the Old Calf Pasture, which includes a boat ramp and auto access from Lowell Road.

Suggested Outings

— Visit Fairhaven Bay
Distance: 2 miles round trip
Portages: None
Parking: Lincoln Canoe Launch, Access 14

— Downstream run of this section
Distance: 7.3 miles
Portages: None
Parking:
    Upstream — Sherman's Bridge Road, Wayland, Access 13
    Downstream — Old Calf Pasture, Concord, Access 15
Note: The near absence of current makes upstream-and-back journeys quite feasible on this river section.

The Assabet River

Rowing our boat against the
current, between wide meadows,
we turn aside into the Assabeth. A
more lovely stream than this, for a
mile above its junction with the
Concord, has never flowed on
earth, — nowhere, indeed, except
to lave the interior of a poet's
imagination. It is sheltered from
the breeze by woods and a hillside;
so that elsewhere there might be a
hurricane, and here scarcely
a ripple across the shaded water.

Nathaniel Hawthorne
Mosses from an Old Manse

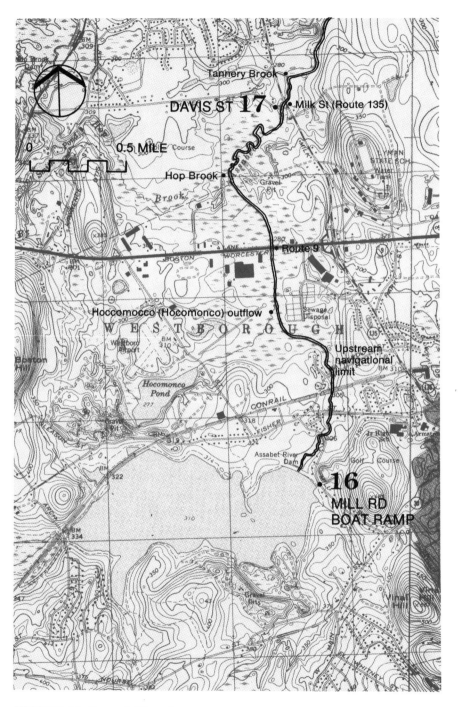

USGS 7.5': Marlborough, Shrewsbury

Assabet River: Towns of Northborough, Westborough

Westborough

Access Points

16 MILL ROAD, Westborough (AS mile 0.0)
USGS Shrewsbury quadrangle
Along the road near the boat ramp there is parking for a
dozen or more automobiles.

17 DAVIS STREET/ROUTE 135(Milk Street), Westborough
(AS mile 2.6)
USGS Shrewsbury quadrangle
Landowner objections and a lack of parking have eliminated a former access point at nearby Davis Street.
At seasons of low vegetation, a convenient alternative is
just south of the Route 135(Milk Street) bridge on the right
bank of the river. Park in the recreation lot 300 yards north
on Route 135. Be careful, there's heavy traffic.

Comments

Assabet Reservoir offers lively still-water canoeing
because few trees were removed before Nichols Dam
flooded the woodland. Dead for two decades, some of the
tree trunks are standing yet. Many of their tops are above
the water, providing bird housing. Other stumps are just
under the surface, all but impossible to see, waiting to
surprise the canoeist. "Stick-ups," as bass fishers call
shafts of standing deadwood, provide underwater cover
for fish, which somehow thrive in these algae-ridden
waters.

This 310-acre impoundment receives its water from
several brooks which drain areas to the south and west in
the towns of Shrewsbury and Grafton. Presumably the
brook with the largest flow could claim the name of
Assabet; however, current usage is that the river begins
with the discharge at Nichols Dam.

The reservoir is part of the overall flood-control plan
for the Concord Basin. It is sometimes called SuAsCo

Reservoir, meaning Sudbury/Assabet/Concord, which gives the false impression that it has something to do with the Sudbury. Occasionally it is referred to as Nichols Reservoir, after its dam. The George H. Nichols Dam, constructed in 1969, is one of a series of flood-control projects built in response to the severe floods and hurricanes of the 1950s. The flood-control function of the dam is to limit the release of water from the upper reaches of the Assabet Basin. Conversely, the reservoir can supply a minimum flow for the river in periods of low water. And the reservoir provides recreation through the creation of a "warm-water fishery." It contains bass, pickerel, sunfish, crappie, and bullheads. The maximum depth is fifteen feet. People fish from the dam and from small boats and canoes. Because of the trees the reservoir is unsuited to speed-boating.

Railroad tracks run along the northwest corner of Assabet Reservoir. The same tracks run beside Cedar Swamp Pond, head of the Sudbury River. The rail line follows the Sudbury's floodplain east until that river turns north, in Ashland.

The best time to canoe Assabet Reservoir is April or May. A visit then allows observation of the nesting behavior of swallows, kingbirds, red-winged blackbirds, yellow warblers, Canada geese, and great blue herons. About twenty pairs of great blue herons nest in the southwest corner of the reservoir. The nests ought be viewed quietly, from a distance, because chicks and eggs are in danger of being bumped from their nests by startled parents. Tree swallows nest in stick-ups throughout the reservoir.

Another advantage of a springtime visit is that large algae blooms cloud the water during the summer. On the other hand, summer droughts allow the formation of mud flats which attract large numbers of shorebirds.

Suggested Outings
— Tour of reservoir perimeter
Distance: 4 miles
Portages: None
Parking: Mill Road, Access 16

— To and from great blue heron nest colony
Distance: 2.5 miles
Portages: None
Parking: Mill Road, Access 16

Great blue herons nest in a colony at Westborough's Assabet Reservoir. Canoeists should observe from a distance, to avoid accidental destruction of eggs and chicks by startled adults.

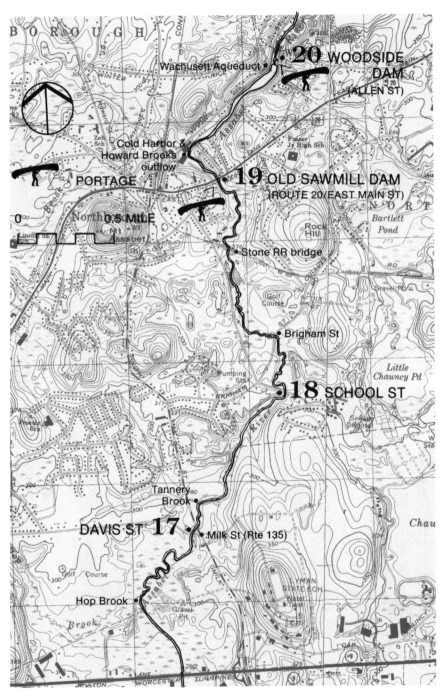

USGS 7.5': Marlborough, Shrewsbury

Assabet River: Towns of Northborough, Westborough

Canoeing the Assabet

Westborough, Northborough

Access Points

17 DAVIS STREET/ROUTE 135(Milk Street), Westborough (AS mile 2.6)
USGS Shrewsbury quadrangle
Landowner objections and a lack of parking have eliminated a former access point at nearby Davis Street.
At seasons of low vegetation, a convenient alternative is just south of the Route 135(Milk Street) bridge on the right bank of the river. Park in the recreation lot 300 yards north on Route 135. Be careful, there's heavy traffic.

18 SCHOOL STREET, Northborough (AS mile 4.1)
USGS Shrewsbury quadrangle
New construction has eliminated this as an access site.

19 OLD SAWMILL DAM, Route 20 (East Main Street) Northborough (AS mile 5.3)
USGS Shrewsbury quadrangle
Commercial parking lots flank the dam. Upstream access is on either side of the river.

20 WOODSIDE DAM, Allen Street, Northborough (AS mile 6.3)
USGS Shrewsbury quadrangle
Put in from the right bank fifty yards below the dam. Park along the street to the right of the river.

Comments

A thorough canoe exploration of the Assabet includes starting from the Route 135 bridge and paddling upstream as far as possible.

During the first part of the upstream journey, the Assabet is the boundary between Westborough and Northborough. Which town you are in depends on which bank of the river is nearer.

Hop Brook (AS mile 2.1) drains the southwest corner of Northborough. In Sudbury there is a different brook with the same name.

The Route 9 bridge (AS mile 1.7) should not be considered an access point, due to the speed of the traffic, the absence of parking, and the difficulty of the put-in.

After paddling under Route 9, you will notice the flatness of the terrain on both sides of the river. This is the bottom of an ancient lake that existed ten to twelve thousand years ago. (See page 103).

The river diminishes upstream of the Westborough Wastewater Treatment Plant at AS mile 1.5, demonstrating the importance of thorough sewage treatment to the quality of the Assabet. This plant receives wastewater from Westborough, Hopkinton, and Shrewsbury. Before the new facility began to operate in 1987, the discharge from the old plant disgusted and dismayed canoeists. The new plant's effluent is relatively clear and odorless.

The Assabet's first major tributary is the outflow from a kettle pond named Hoccomocco, also spelled Hoccomonco, (AS mile 1.3). Its exact point of entrance is obscured by the swampy river border. Hoccomocco suffers from creosote pollution, the legacy of a wood-treatment plant that operated next to it in the first half of the century. Cleanup is planned.

Upstream explorations come to a halt at about AS mile 1.0, due to the woody shrubs that grow over the water, barricading the stream. Compared to the upstream paddle, it takes little effort to shoot down past the wastewater treatment plant, Route 9, and Hop Brook. A June visit produced sightings of eastern kingbirds, gray catbirds, a red-tailed hawk, and a great blue heron, plus damselflies, dragonflies, and many other insects.

The put-in at the Route 135 bridge might be the end of an exploration of the uppermost reaches of the Assabet...or you may continue downriver to Northborough.

Tannery Brook (AS mile 2.8) once flushed wastes from Phineas Davis's tannery. In 1778, when Davis went into the business, hides were turned into leather by prolonged soaking in a solution of tannin, which was obtained from the bark of hemlock or other trees, or from the rhizomes of yellow pond lilies. Abundant tannin in the swampy sources of the Assabet and the Sudbury gives their waters a naturally brownish hue.

Shortly past a hill the town boundary leads to the right, leaving the canoeist completely in Northborough. The banks come nearer to the stream, and the current picks up. School Street crosses at AS mile 4.1. The culverts under Brigham Street (AS mile 4.6, no parking) lead into the Juniper Hill Golf Course. In the golf course my canoe disturbed four mallards, which leaped into flight. Through the wake of their wingbeats flew a solitary swallow, to seize a white feather shed by one of the ducks. Tree swallows line their nest with feathers, so this was a prize for the agile little bird.

The bridges provided for golf carts require some ducking. Just beyond the golf course a slough or backwater connects to the river. In this place a scoop with a dip net produced a giant water bug with eggs cemented to his back. (See page 196.)

The stone railroad bridge (AS mile 5.0) supports tracks that connect Northborough with the big Conrail complex near Farm Pond in Framingham. Beneath this bridge, the current is brisk and the channel shallow. Downstream, the narrow river is at some points obstructed with shrubs, making passage difficult at some water levels.

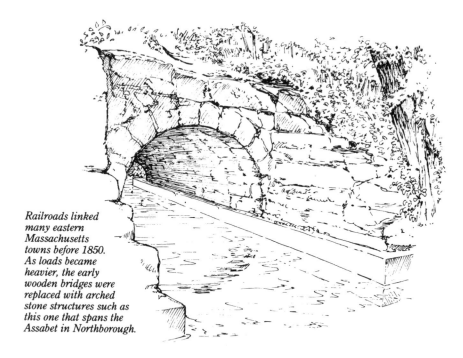

Railroads linked many eastern Massachusetts towns before 1850. As loads became heavier, the early wooden bridges were replaced with arched stone structures such as this one that spans the Assabet in Northborough.

The Old Sawmill Dam is just upstream of Route 20 (Main Street) in Northborough. It was built in 1855 and is fifteen feet high. The original dam, built in 1751, powered Samuel Wood's fulling mill. (See page 111.) Iron, shoes, rifles, bonemeal, and tortoise shell buttons were manufactured here at various times during the nineteenth century.

Take out above the dam into one of the parking lots on either side of the river. If continuing downstream, portage across Route 20. Access is on the left fifty yards below the bridge.

Suggested Outings
— Davis Street/Route 135(Milk Street), Westborough, up-stream 1.6 miles and return to start.
Distance: 3.2 miles round trip
Portages: None
Parking: Northborough Parks and Recreation lot, Access 17

— Davis Street/Route 135(Milk Street), Westborough down-stream to Route 20 in Northborough.
Distance: 2.7 miles
Portages: None
Parking:
    Upstream — Northborough Parks and Recreation lot, Access 17
    Downstream — Old Sawmill Dam, Access 19

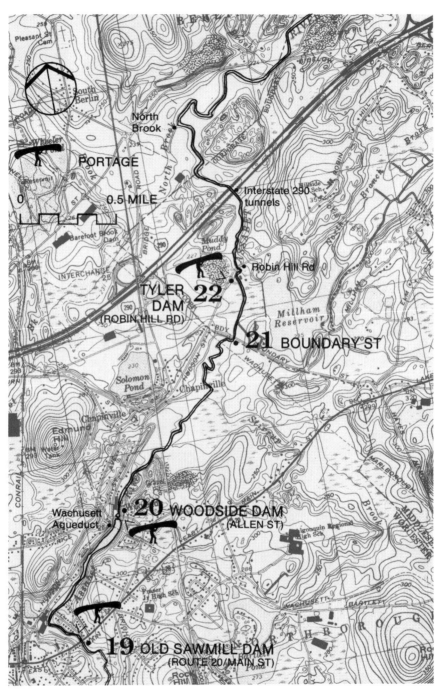

PORTAGE

0   0.5 MILE

North
Brook

Interstate 290
tunnels

Muddy
Pond

Robin Hill Rd

TYLER **22**
DAM
(ROBIN HILL RD)

Millham
Reservoir

21 BOUNDARY ST

Solomon
Pond

Chapinville

Wachusett
Aqueduct **20** WOODSIDE DAM
(ALLEN ST)

19 OLD SAWMILL DAM
(ROUTE 20/MAIN ST)

USGS 7.5': Hudson, Marlborough

Assabet River: Towns of Berlin, Northborough; City of Marlborough

Canoeing the Assabet

Northborough, Marlborough, Berlin, Hudson

Access Points

19 OLD SAWMILL DAM, Route 20 (East Main Street),
Northborough (AS mile 5.3)
USGS Shrewsbury quadrangle
The river is reached from the left bank just downstream
from the Route 20 bridge. Park, with permission, in one
of the commercial lots in the neighborhood.

20 WOODSIDE DAM, Allen Street, Northborough (AS mile
6.3)
USGS Shrewsbury quadrangle
Put in from the right bank fifty yards below the dam.
Park along the street to the right of the river.

21 BOUNDARY STREET, on the Marlborough-
Northborough border. (AS mile 7.6)
USGS Marlborough quadrangle
Park along Boundary Street. Access is on the right above
the bridge.

22 TYLER DAM, Robin Hill Road, Marlborough (AS mile
8.0)
USGS Marlborough quadrangle
Park along the road. Be careful to avoid blocking Hillside
Farm vehicles. River access is in the slough below the
dam.

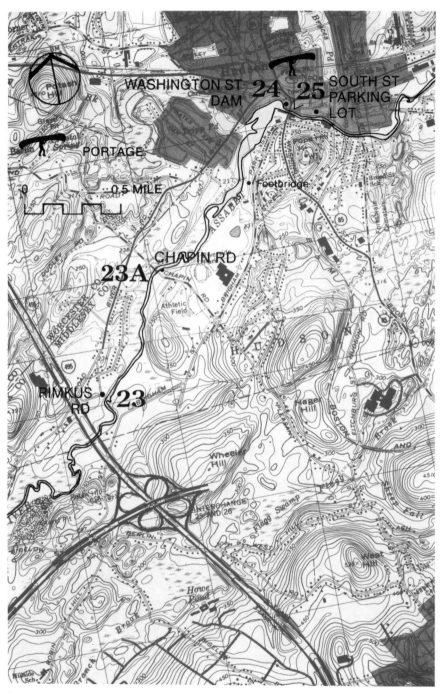

WASHINGTON ST
DAM

PORTAGE

0   0.5 MILE

24 25 SOUTH ST
         PARKING
         LOT

Footbridge

CHAPIN RD

23A

RIMKUS
RD 23

USGS 7.5': *Hudson, Marlborough*

Assabet River: Towns of Berlin, Hudson; City of Marlborough

23 RIMKUS ROAD, Hudson (AS mile 11.4)
USGS Marlborough quadrangle
Behind the graffiti-covered town well building, a path
leads down to the river, offering excellent access.

23A CHAPIN ROAD, Hudson (AS mile 12.2)
USGS Hudson quadrangle
A new access is on the right bank of the river down
stream from the Chapin Road bridge, with off-road
parking for four to six cars.

24 WASHINGTON STREET DAM, Hudson (AS mile 13.6)
USGS Hudson quadrangle
Upstream access is from the left bank in the municipal
parking lot behind Hudson Library. See notes below for
instructions on the portage to the downstream access.

25 SOUTH STREET PARKING LOT, Hudson (AS mile 13.8)
USGS Hudson quadrangle
Access is at the rear of this large parking lot.

Comments
Below the Old Sawmill Dam access, a mill complex is on the
left, which was powered by water from Howard Brook and
Cold Harbor Brook. Their combined discharge enters the
Assabet from beneath the mill building (AS mile 5.5). These
two brooks drain wide expanses of woodland and orchard in
western and northern Northborough. They are stocked with
trout in the springtime.

Just past the mill is River Street. The current slows as it
feels the influence of Woodside Dam. Wachusett Aqueduct (AS
mile 6.3) crosses the narrow impoundment on seven high
stone arches just above Woodside Dam. This is a good place to
fish.

To portage, take out on the right bank, above Allen Street
Bridge, which is just upstream from the dam. A carry of one
hundred yards along the right bank reaches a trail down to the
river. Watch for poison ivy.

Woodside Dam was built in 1851 by David Wood to power
his mill. The large mill building, which spans the river, is being
converted into apartments. This is the only building that goes
across one of our rivers. It was built in 1888.

Below the dam, the current is swift, and there are some rocks to be avoided. About a half-mile down (AS mile 6.8) a log crosses the river. It is a *hazard* in high water.

Stirrup Brook (AS mile 7.3) enters from the right. It is stocked with trout, some of which find their way into the Assabet. The river winds through fields in the floodplain. Bass lurk in the outsides of the bends.

Just past Boundary Street (AS mile 7.6) effluent from Marlborough's Westerly Wastewater Treatment Plant enters on the right.

At AS mile 8.0, a mass of earth and concrete confronts the canoeist: the Tyler flood-control dam. If you were a fish or a muskrat you could swim through a pipe in the base of the dam. In normal conditions this culvert conducts the whole Assabet. At flood stage, the culvert would not be large enough for all the water, which would back up and deepen until it reached a set of intakes. These are over a canoeist's head when the river is within its banks. If the water were high enough to reach these intakes, the broad state-owned floodplain through which you just canoed would be a sizable lake. If the water continued to deepen, it would at last pour over a spillway in the dam.

The dam's effect on flooding of the lower Assabet and the Concord is a subject of controversy. By delaying the discharge of Assabet floodwater, the dam may *raise* the downstream flood crest, by causing the highest water from the Assabet to combine with that from the slower-flowing Sudbury.

Carry out on the left. From the top of the dam you can see a slough projecting from the pool below the dam. This is a good place to put in.

Robin Hill Road, in Marlborough, crosses just below the dam. The small I-beams under this bridge provide just enough ledge to accommodate barn swallow nests, and are thoroughly exploited by these graceful birds.

Below the bridge, the banks are forested. The trees are hemlock, white ash, and white pine. Shrubs include elderberry and arrowwood. By late summer, the riverbed is covered with pondweed and water celery. The river passes under Interstate 290 (AS mile 8.6) via two long concrete tunnels and through a corner of Berlin (AS mile 8.8). Where the Assabet nears River Road are stands of big white pines and open meadows.

Bigelow Road (AS mile 9.8) has no shoulder or pulloff, so does not offer convenient access. A fifth of a mile below, a marsh spreads to the left. Small birches toss on the right bank.

The river winds through another mile of Marlborough before it finally enters Hudson (AS mile 10.8). From here the Assabet has frequent backwaters or sloughs — fingers of water that point upstream. What a cradle these sloughs offer to aquatic life! They are full of feisty little fish, mostly bass and pickerel, which live on the bountiful supply of invertebrates found in the warm, still water.

A Volkswagen beetle is under the Assabet just upstream of Interstate 495 (AS mile 11.1). Just downstream is the Assabet's finest tree house, reaching out over a backwater. It was built by a consortium of neighborhood kids. They should have a reception for Assabet River canoeists.

Below the tree house the river divides and shoots through two openings in a dike-like structure. On the left the Rimkus Road access point (AS mile 11.4) is under the power line. A short trail leads up to the street.

After a long straight stretch the river reaches Chapin Road (AS mile 12.2). Riverside Park borders the river in Hudson. Fish-laden backwaters continue. Past the foot-bridge (AS mile 13.3) the river widens into a lake. The takeout is at the end of this stretch of stillwater on the left bank of the river, to the left of the cannon.

If continuing downstream to Gleasondale, a portage of three blocks through downtown Hudson is necessary. Take out at the parking lot behind the fire station, carry past the cannon, and cross Veteran's Park between the library and the church. Turn right and carry down the sidewalk. Cross Route 85 (Washington Street). Turn left onto South Street at the service station. Continue a block and a half, to the large parking lot on the right. Put in from the rear edge of the parking lot, which is on the left bank of the river.

Suggested Outings
— Hudson's Washington Street Dam, upstream and back.
Still water behind the Hudson dam winds through
Riverside Park, making this a good trip for beginners.
Canoes can be rented from the Fishing Tackle Annex
next to the parking lot.
Distance: Variable
Portages: None below Tyler Dam
Parking: Municipal parking lot at Access 24.

— From Boundary Street upstream toward Northborough
and back. Above Boundary Street the Assabet meanders
away from auto traffic through agricultural land well
worthy of exploration in high water.
Distance: 2 miles round trip
Portages: None
Parking: Along Boundary Street, Access 21

— Downstream from Tyler Dam to Washington Street
Dam.
Distance: 5.6 miles
Portages: None
Parking:
    Upstream — Along street to right of river,
    Access 20.
    Downstream — In municipal lot at library,
    Access 24

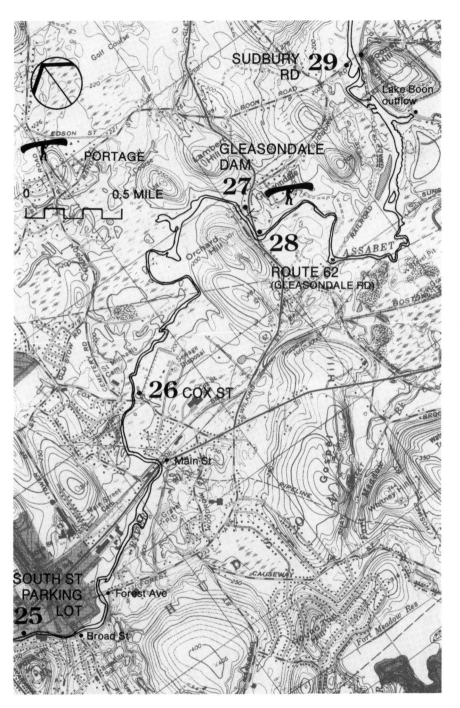

USGS 7.5': Hudson, Marlborough
Assabet River: Towns of Hudson, Stow

Canoeing the Assabet

Hudson, Stow, Maynard

Access Points

25 SOUTH STREET PARKING LOT, Hudson (AS mile 13.8)
USGS Hudson quadrangle
Access is at the rear of this large parking lot.

26 COX STREET, Hudson (AS mile 15.6)
USGS Hudson quadrangle
Access is downstream of the bridge, on the right bank.
There is parking for several cars along the road.

27 GLEASONDALE DAM, Stow (AS mile 17.4)
USGS Hudson quadrangle
There is no good takeout above the dam. Private homes
line the left bank and there is no portage route or road
access on the right bank. It's best to enjoy another view of
Orchard Hill as you paddle back to Cox Street.

28 ROUTE 62 (Gleasondale Road), Stow (AS mile 17.8)
USGS Hudson quadrangle
To begin a downstream trip at Gleasondale, put in from
the downstream side of the Route 62 bridge. There is
limited on-road parking.

29 SUDBURY ROAD, Stow (AS mile 20.3)
USGS Hudson quadrangle
Both ends of the bridge have parking and access on the
upstream side.

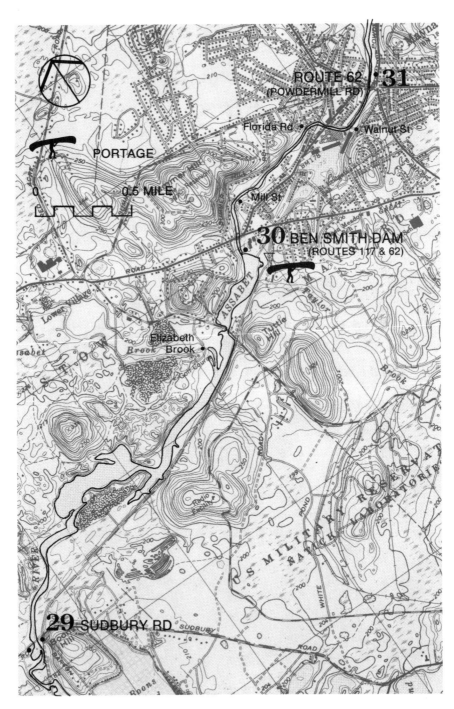

ROUTE 62 •31
(POWDERMILL RD)

Florida Rd • • •Walnut St

PORTAGE

0   0.5 MILE

Mill St •

30 BEN SMITH DAM
(ROUTES 117 & 62)

ASSABET

Elizabeth
Brook   Brook •

29 SUDBURY RD

USGS 7.5': Hudson, Maynard

Assabet River: Towns of Maynard, Stow

29 SUDBURY ROAD, Stow (AS mile 20.3)
USGS Hudson quadrangle
Both ends of the bridge have parking and access on the
upstream side.

30 BEN SMITH DAM, Maynard (also called American
Woolen Dam((AS mile 22.7)
USGS Maynard quadrangle
The Mill Pond Building parking lot, adjacent to the dam
on the right side of the river, offers easy access above
and below the dam.

31 ROUTE 62, Powder Mill Road, one tenth of a mile
northeast of the intersection with Route 27, Maynard
(AS mile 24.3)
USGS Maynard quadrangle
The river is reached at the rear of this capacious
parking lot.

Comments
If you are beginning a downstream run from the center of
Hudson, duck! Shortly after putting in from the South
Street parking lot, Houghton Street crosses on a low bridge
(AS mile 14.0). The pipes beneath the bridge are low and
potentially hazardous. Two more bridges cross in quick suc-
cession, Broad Street (AS mile 14.2) and Forest Avenue (AS
mile 14.5). In late spring, watch for yellow iris.

Main Street/Route 62 (AS mile 15.2) has railroad
bridges just above and below it. Their trestles snag obstructions. Just below Cox Street (AS mile 15.6) fallen trees have
the same effect. The Hudson Wastewater Treatment Plant
(AS mile 16.0) marks the halfway point of the Assabet.
Beyond is a particularly nice stretch that lies upstream of
the Stow village of Gleasondale.

At the Stow boundary (AS mile 16.3) the river makes a
sharp left turn to swing north of Orchard Hill. This nearly
treeless hill creates a striking landscape. It is a drumlin, a
hill composed of clay and boulders rolled into a lump by glacial action. At the summit of Orchard Hill is a meltwater

channel, eroded from the top of the hill during the glacial era by water flowing down through the ice above. The grass of Orchard Hill provides a hundred acres of habitat for bobolinks, which need undisturbed grassland for nesting. Kestrels are often seen here.

On the left bank of the river is a golf course, the first course in the country open to African-American golfers. It was built by Charles Cox in the 1920s. Originally called Mapledale, it was a popular recreational facility for years. The first national black tournament was played here in 1926. The course is now owned by Stow Acres Country Club.

The golf course was once the country seat of the Randall family. Dr. John Witt Randall, born in 1813, was a naturalist and a great grandson of Samuel Adams.

Dr. Randall wrote a long poem about the Assabet. After verses praising the Assabet's tranquillity, the poem continues:

> Oft does lose thy tranquil look
> Destined in a sterner course
> Force to overcome with force.
> When beneath a three days shower
> Driven before the freshet's power
> Who shall dare thy waves restrain
> Lashed along by wind and rain.

Canoeists take heed!

Past the golf course, fine houses built by the Gleasondale mill owners overlook the river. They are inhabited by descendants of B.W. Gleason, the entrepreneur who, with his partner Samuel J. Dale, purchased a woolen mill on this site in 1849, saw it burn, and built the brick one in 1854.

Gleasondale was formerly known as Rock Bottom. Rock Bottom on the Assabet River provided much fodder for low jests by vaudeville comedians. In 1898 citizens successfully petitioned the postmaster to change the name of their post office to Gleasondale.

The portage around the dam at Gleasondale must be scouted and negotiated cautiously. Conditions and preferred routes vary according to the water level and the dispositions of landowners. Good access to deep water is found below the Route 62 bridge.

Downstream from Gleasondale, streamside vegetation includes a nice variety of freshwater plants: wild rice, burreed, arrowwood, bulrushes, jewelweed, arrowhead, pickerelweed, cattails, buttonbush, and purple loosestrife.

The outflow from Lake Boon (AS mile 19.9) enters through a wide channel on the right. From 1906 through the 1930s, steamboats carried people from Maynard up the Assabet to Whitman's Crossing, near the present Sudbury Road bridge (AS mile 20.3). After walking to Lake Boon, people could tour it in the motor launch Princess. Although it is known locally as Lake Boon, the United States Geological Survey's official designation is Boons Pond.

Past Sudbury Road the river becomes deeper and slower. Military property called the Fort Devens Annex borders the right bank for several miles. According to one naturalist, there is an active beaver colony in this inaccessible area.

On the left is the Gardner Hill Conservation Land in Stow, which is a fine place to picnic.

Elizabeth Brook (AS mile 22.3) is also referred to as Assabet Brook. The name of the Assabet River suffered from similar confusion until 1850. Assabet, Asebath, Asibath, Elsibethe, Elizabeth were variations in the English phonetization of the Nipmuck name for the river. Elizabeth Brook drops 250 feet from a bog in Harvard to the point at which it joins the Assabet.

Near the boundary between Stow and Hudson, the Assabet River winds around a drumlin called Orchard Hill.

The Maynard boundary is at Russell's Bridge just beyond Stow Away Golf Club. After a paddle down its impoundment, Ben Smith Dam is approached, *with caution,* at AS mile 22.7. Take out on the right, well above the dam.

Suggested Outings
— From Cox Street, Hudson, to Gleasondale, Stow. Return to start. This beautiful stretch of the Assabet winds around three sides of Orchard Hill. On the return trip, the current may pose stiff opposition.
Distance: 3.6 miles round trip
Portages: None
Parking: Access 26

— From Gleasondale, Stow, to Ben Smith Dam, Maynard
Distance: 4.9 miles
Portages: None
Parking:
    Upstream — Beside Route 62, Access 27
    Downstream — Parking lot near dam, Access 30

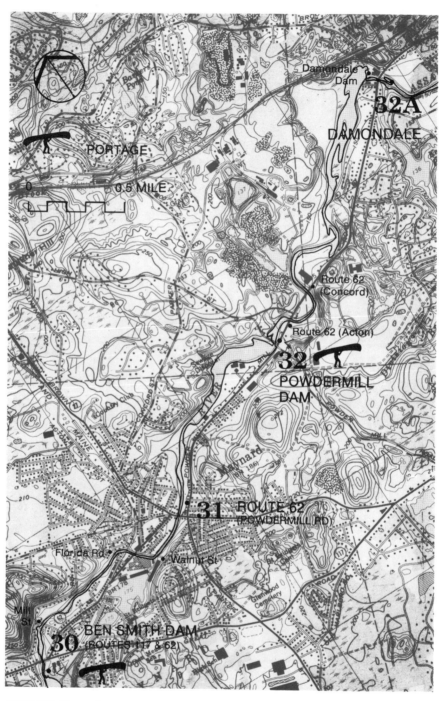

USGS 7.5': Maynard

Assabet River: Towns of Acton, Concord, Maynard, Sudbury

Maynard, Acton, Concord

Access Points

30 BEN SMITH DAM (Routes 117 and 62), Maynard (also called American Woolen Dam) (AS mile 22.7)
USGS Maynard quadrangle
The Mill Pond Building parking lot, adjacent to the dam on the right side of the river, offers easy access above and below the dam.

31 ROUTE 62 (Powder Mill Road), Maynard one tenth of a mile northeast of the intersection with Route 27 (AS mile 24.3)
USGS Maynard quadrangle
The river is reached at the rear of this capacious parking lot.

32 POWDERMILL DAM, Acton (also called Prescott Dam and High Street Dam) (AS mile 25.3)
USGS Maynard quadrangle
The river may be reached upstream of the dam (not recommended for canoeing) and immediately downstream of the mill buildings on Route 62. Park with permission at the mill buildings.

32A DAMONDALE, West Concord (AS mile 27.2)
USGS Maynard quadrangle
River access with parking for four cars is available at the entrance to Westvale Glen, a condominium development across Route 62 from Damonmill Square. A path from the parking area leads to the launch site at the end of the old power canal for the mill, just before it joins the river.

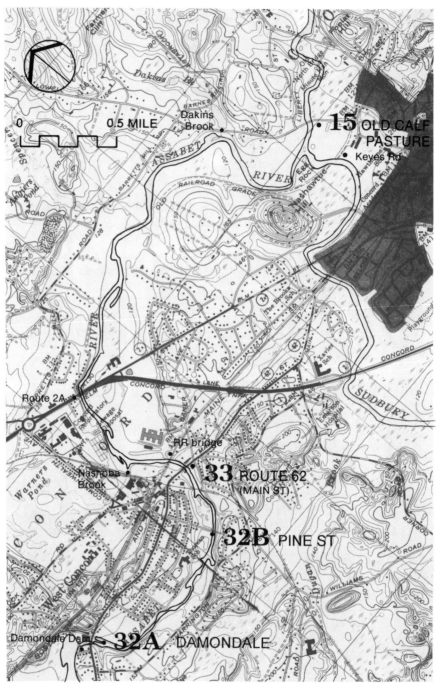

USGS 7.5': Concord, Maynard
Assabet River: Town of Concord

32B PINE STREET BRIDGE, West Concord (AS mile 28.1)
  USGS Maynard quadrangle
  Access is on the left bank, upstream from the bridge.
  There is parking for several cars.

33 ROUTE 62 (Main Street), West Concord (AS mile 28.5)
  USGS Maynard quadrangle
  Access is to the river's right, upstream of the bridge.
  Load or unload cars in the small parking lot beside the
  river, but park in the large lot kitty corner to the launch
  site - across Route 62 and across the river.

15 OLD CALF PASTURE, Lowell Road, Concord
  (AS mile 31.9; SU mile 31.2; CO mile 0.1)
  USGS Concord quadrangle
  A boat ramp and parking for about six cars are provided
  at the Old Calf Pasture Conservation Area, which is on
  the right bank of the river, just upstream from Lowell
  Road.

Comments

In 1847, Amory Maynard bought land from a farmer
named Smith, and built a dam at a place called Assabet
Village. He built mills powered with Assabet water. By
1900, the United States had no larger woolen mills than
those at Maynard, as the town was called after 1871.
The mill buildings, now known as Clock Tower Place,
house a number of small companies and organizations,
including Sudbury Valley Trustees.

Bedrock is exposed at the dam. The stone is granite
porphyry. This rock slowly crystallized from magma while
it lay eight or more miles below the surface. Because it
cooled so slowly, large crystals formed. A fresh surface
has the spotted appearance of raisin bread. This is not
visible on the surface of the exposure because it has been
discolored by reactions with air and water, and is covered
with moss and lichen.

Below Ben Smith Dam the Assabet tumbles through
Maynard. To flatwater canoeists, the rapids look intimidat-
ing or altogether impossible. Those trained for white
water are less impressed with the difficulties. The hazards
should not be underestimated, but those with proper
preparation can canoe through Maynard at times of high
water.

The Assabet flows beneath two street bridges, makes a sharp right turn, goes under a new foot bridge, under Route 62, and then reaches its greatest hazard. At the second Route 62 crossing (Main Street, AS mile 23.7) the river bends sharply to the left. On the outside of the turn, a torrent pours down from above the level of the river. An out-of-control canoe could be swamped by the water, and boat and occupants held below the surface by its force. This is Assabet water, taken above Ben Smith Dam through a sluiceway, now rejoining the river.

From here there is one more bridge, Routes 27 and 62, where there is a USGS gauging station. The average annual flow at this point is 195 cubic feet per second. After a stretch of flatwater, Access 31 is reached at the large parking lot (AS 24.3) on the right bank.

From this point the Assabet is tamer, though not without excitement. The current is slowed by the Powder Mill Dam. The river enters the southern tip of Acton. In the recent past this part of the Assabet was closed to boating because sludge from a primitive wastewater treatment plant accumulated behind the dam, feeding great concentrations of bacteria. The recent upgrading of the Maynard wastewater treatment plant drastically improved the situation, but the pond above the dam is still not recommended to the canoeist.

In 1835 Nathan Pratt built the first gunpowder mill at this location (AS mile 25.3). There appears to have been a tendency for these mills to explode. From Thoreau's *Journal*, July 21, 1859:

> As you draw near the powder-mills, you see the hill behind bestrewn with the fragments of mills which have blown up in past years, the fragments of the millers having been removed, and the canal is cluttered with the larger ruins. The very river makes greater haste past the dry-house, as it were for fear of accident.

After World War I the last powder mill closed. The site was converted to the production of electricity in the 1920s. The falling Assabet generates kilowatts here today.

To portage, take out on the right bank above the dam and bridge, carry around the mill buildings, and put in just below (AS mile 25.4).

The river crisscrosses Route 62, which follows the Assabet's valley but not its meanders. The first bridge is in Acton (AS mile 25.5) and the next in Concord one-fifth of a mile below. The water is shallow quickwater, pleasant if the flow is sufficient, scratchy or worse in low water.

The river rushes through a broken dam at the mill at Damondale in West Concord (AS mile 27.2). Take out above the dam to scout. Make sure the chute through the dam is clear of obstructions, and plan the best route between the stones downstream.

Route 62 crosses again just below the mill. For the rest of its length the Assabet maintains a steady current, slowing somewhat in the deepening channel. Large trees shade the river. Kingfishers find this a particularly attractive area.

At a gray stone bridge (AS mile 28.5) there is a convenient take out on the right bank. This is the upstream terminus of the outing suggested below. If you are trustful enough to leave your canoe, you can cross the river on the bridge, cross the road, and buy ice cream in a commercial strip. Abruptly leaving the realm of the river for a brief return to the world of autos and air conditioning gives one an odd sensation. It seems fitting to compare these worlds and to enjoy them both, because the river's health and beauty does not depend on a political contest between industrial and environmental values. The Assabet's future depends on a consensus that maintains clean water *and* industrial production.

The Assabet River meets the Sudbury River at Egg Rock in Concord, to form the Concord River.

Nashoba Brook (AS mile 28.7) drains eastern Acton. Odoriferous wastewater enters from the same side a fifth of a mile farther along. Fortunately its effect is soon diluted by the now substantial Assabet. A state prison (MCI Concord) is on the left bank. Route 2A (AS mile 28.9) is this river's last bridge.

Dakins Brook (AS mile 30.0) lies just beyond Willow Island. The river turns south around Dove Rock. The historic lower Assabet contains, at a location known as the Leaning Hemlocks (AS mile 31.5), a plaque in the memory of the nineteenth-century outdoorsman George Bartlett, an organizer of many river outings. Overlooking the plaque to the southwest is Nashawtuc Hill.

The Assabet River is the senior partner in the Concord, discharging more water than the Sudbury River. They join at Egg Rock (AS mile 31.8). The boat ramp at the Old Calf Pasture is just downstream on the right.

Suggested Outing
— Upstream and back, from Old Calf Pasture to Route 62, Main Street, West Concord. Heading upstream from Egg Rock, the first bridge encountered is Route 2A. Farther upstream is a railroad bridge. The next auto bridge is the upstream terminus.
Distance: 6.8 miles round trip
Portages: None
Parking: At Old Calf Pasture, Access 15

The Concord River

*Concord River is remarkable for the gentleness of
its current, which is scarcely perceptible, and
some have referred to its influence the proverbial
moderation of the inhabitants of Concord, as
exhibited in the Revolution, and on later
occasions. It has been proposed that the town
should adopt for its coat of arms a field verdant,
with the Concord circling nine times round. I
have read that a descent of an eighth of an inch
in a mile is sufficient to produce a flow. Our
river has, probably, very near the smallest
allowance. The story is current, at any rate,
though I believe that strict history will not bear
it out, that the only bridge ever carried away on
the main branch within the limits of the town, was
driven up stream by the wind.*

Henry David Thoreau
A Week on the Concord and Merrimack Rivers

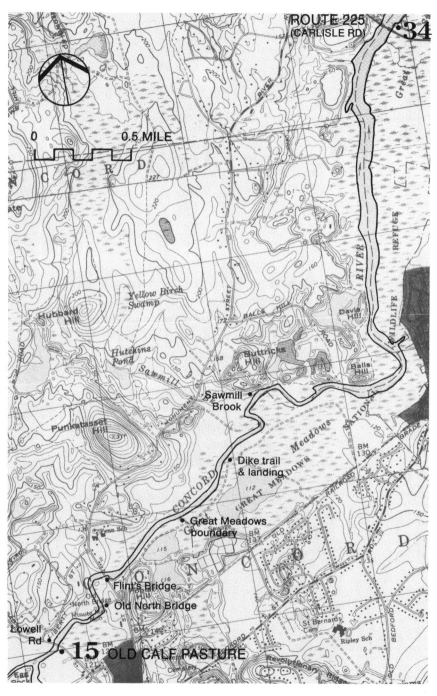

0   0.5 MILE

CONCORD

Yellow Birch
Swamp

Hubbard
Hill

Hutchins
Pond

Sawmill

Punkatasset
Hill

BALLS HILL

Buttricks
Hill

Davis
Hill

Balls
Hill

WILDLIFE REFUGE

GREAT

RIVER

Meadows

GREAT MEADOWS

Sawmill
Brook

Dike trail
& landing

Great Meadows
boundary

CONCORD

BM
130

BM
137

Flint's Bridge

Old North Bridge

Lowell
Rd

·15 BM

OLD CALF PASTURE

C   O   R   D

St Bernards
Cem

Ripley Sch

BEDFORD

USGS 7.5': *Billerica, Concord*

Concord River: Towns of Bedford, Carlisle, Concord

Canoeing the Concord

Concord, Bedford

Access Points

15 OLD CALF PASTURE. Lowell Road, Concord
(CO mile 0.1; SU mile 31.2; AS mile 31.9)
USGS Concord quadrangle
A boat ramp and parking for about six cars are provided
at the Old Calf Pasture Conservation Area, which is on
the right bank of the river, just upstream from Lowell
Road.

34 ROUTE 225 (Carlisle Road), Bedford
(CO mile 4.5)
USGS Billerica quadrangle
Bedford Boat Ramp is downstream of the Carlisle Road
bridge, on the right bank. A large number of cars may be
parked here.
If the boat ramp is closed, river access is available at the
old bridge abutment on the left bank, where five or six
cars may be parked.

Comments

Putting in from the Old Calf Pasture, one soon passes the
Old Manse and goes under Old North Bridge. It would
seem appropriate to be paddling an Old Town canoe. The
town of Concord has played such a role in American
history and letters that it may be permitted some quaint-
ness. Emerson, Thoreau, Hawthorne and the Alcotts
didn't come to Concord on purpose to become renowned

writers; Concord was their home, and they wrote. That the same town was the site of the famous battle a few decades earlier is a remarkable coincidence.

The Old Manse (CO mile 0.3) is on the right bank, set back from the river. It was built in 1770 by Rev. William Emerson, grandfather of Ralph Waldo Emerson. The elder Emerson watched the North Bridge skirmish from an upstairs window. Ralph Waldo Emerson wrote *Nature* in this house. Newlyweds Nathaniel Hawthorne and Sophia Peabody began their passionate marriage here in 1842. In the late 19th century, George Bartlett had a boathouse behind the Old Manse, which served as headquarters for the river outings he organized, and in which he wrote a guide book, poems, and articles about the river. The naturalist William Brewster began his residence in Concord by taking rooms in the Manse in 1886. Brewster was the first president of Massachusetts Audubon Society, which was the first Audubon Society in the country.

The Old North Bridge replica (CO mile 0.5) is in Minuteman National Historic Park. On April 19, 1775, British troops had marched out from Boston to confiscate military supplies stored in Concord. A detachment of British soldiers was sent from the center of town to guard the bridge. Minutemen on the high ground to the left of the river saw smoke from the village center. Believing that the British were firing the town, the Minutemen decided to force their way across the bridge. The British guards fired from the bridgehead and the Minutemen returned fire. There were casualties on both sides. The surviving British retreated to the village.

Minutemen continued to stream toward Concord from all directions. By the time the red-coated column began its withdrawal toward Boston, it was surrounded by hostile colonial militia. The ensuing bloody fight was the beginning of America's war for independence.

Daniel Chester French's minuteman statue is at one approach to the bridge. It bears Emerson's inscription:

By the rude bridge that arched the flood,
Their flag to April's breeze unfurled,
Here once the embattled farmers stood,
And fired the shot heard round the world.

Just past the bridge, a large brick building stands on high ground to the left. This house was built in 1911 by a descendant of John Buttrick who commanded the Acton Minutemen in 1775. The house is now the Park Service's North Bridge Visitors Center. It is open 8:30 A.M. to 5:00 P.M., seven days a week.

Monument Street crosses Flint's Bridge (CO mile 0.7). A sign on this bridge warns motorboaters of the 10 m.p.h. speed limit.

The boundary of Great Meadows National Wildlife Refuge (CO mile 1.2) is marked by a sign. The Concord section of Great Meadows National Wildlife Refuge is on the right bank only, encompassing the marshes and ponds known as Great Meadows. The marshes along the Sudbury are the Broad Meadows. Both marshes were said to be drier prior to the construction of the dam at North Billerica.

Part of Great Meadows was purchased by a hunter named Samuel Hoar in 1928. He built dikes to improve the marsh as habitat for waterfowl. In 1944, he donated 250 acres to the U.S. Fish and Wildlife Service, and that area was incorporated into Great Meadows National Wildlife Refuge.

Great Meadows is one of the outstanding birdwatching locations in New England. Many species of waterfowl can be seen here, particularly in spring and fall. The 1.7-mile Dike Trail runs around one of the marsh ponds. Where it parallels the right bank of the river, it can be reached from several informal points of access, and at the official landing (CO mile 1.7).

At the end of August, 1839, Thoreau boated down the Concord, the trip he described in *A Week on the Concord and Merrimack Rivers.* He wrote: "The Great Meadows, like a broad moccasin print, have levelled a fertile and juicy place in nature." Thoreau enjoyed the blooms of pickerelweed and the occasional cardinal flower along this stretch, and in late summer, you can too.

Along the left bank are several water intakes for the irrigation of the large working farm that stretches for a mile along the left bank, opposite Great Meadows National Wildlife Refuge. From here to Lowell the Concord offers fine habitat for painted turtles, which climb onto every available perch to sun themselves. The small ones are sometimes allowed to bask atop the large ones.

Where the trees along the right bank give way, Great Meadows may be viewed from the river.

Sawmill Brook (CO mile 2.0) enters from the left. Here is the hill the USGS map calls Buttricks. William Brewster refers to it as Holden's Hill. In his journal entry for March 19, 1909, Brewster notes that red-shouldered hawks had returned to the tall chestnut tree on Holden's Hill, in which they had nested the previous two seasons.

Red-shouldered hawks were driven from our area in the 1950s by the pesticide DDT, which has since been banned. Tall chestnuts are also gone, killed by a fungus introduced in New York City in 1904, which eliminated mature trees from the eastern states by 1940, though chestnut sprouts may still be found. Migrant red-shouldered hawks appear from time to time; perhaps one day they will again nest near the Concord River.

Ball's Hill (CO mile 2.2) is next, also on the left. William Brewster built a cabin on the southeast slope, after he purchased the hill in 1891. During the autumns of 1903 and 1904, E.H. Forbush lived in this cabin. Forbush was later Massachusetts' state ornithologist and author of *Birds of Massachusetts and Other New England States.*

Thoreau observed that the river ran perfectly straight for the interval between Ball's Hill and the Carlisle Road bridge (CO mile 4.5) Downstream from Ball's Hill, the town of Bedford is on the right bank. Protected by Great Meadows National Wildlife Refuge, this land remains in marsh and forest. Lavish private homes are scattered along the left bank.

This is a fine section of the river for the observation and photographing of herons.

The Route 225 access (CO miles 4.5) is just below the Carlisle Road bridge.

Suggested Outing
— Downstream through this section.
Distance: 4.4 miles
Portages: none
Parking:
    Upstream — Old Calf Pasture, Access 15
    Downstream — Route 225, Access 34

Note: The current is not swift. This section may be canoed on a round-trip basis.

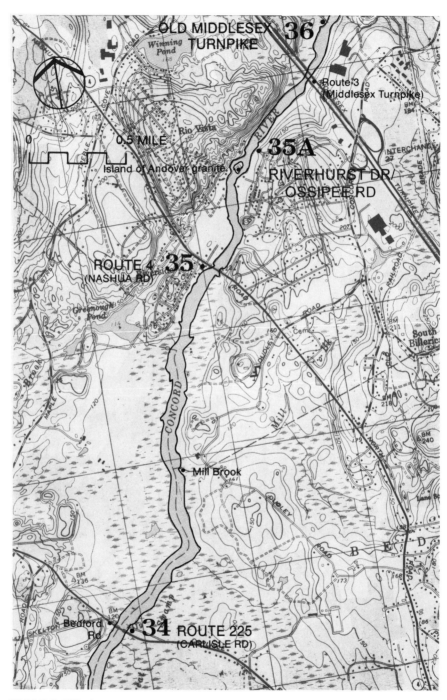

OLD MIDDLESEX TURNPIKE **36**

Route 3
(Middlesex Turnpike)

Winning
Pond

Rio Vista

0   0.5 MILE

Island of Andover granite. **35A**

RIVERHURST DR/
OSSIPEE RD

INTERCHANGE

ROUTE 4 **35**
(NASHUA RD)

Greenough
Pond

CONCORD

South
Billerica

Mill Brook

Mill

B   E   D

Bedford
Rd **34** ROUTE 225
(CARLISLE RD)

USGS 7.5': Billerica

Concord River: Towns of Bedford, Billerica, Carlisle

Bedford, Carlisle, Billerica

Access Points

34 Route 225 (Carlisle Road), Bedford (CO mile 4.5)
USGS Billerica quadrangle
Bedford Boat Ramp is downstream of the Carlisle Road bridge, on the right bank A large number of cars may be parked there.

If the boat ramp is closed, river access is available at the old bridge abutment on the left bank, where five or six cars may be parked.

35 ROUTE 4 (Nashua Road), Billerica (CO mile 6.6)
USGS Billerica quadrangle
Although the gravel embankment on the left bank, upstream of the bridge, offers river access, the adjacent parking lot is reserved for restaurant patrons. The nearby marina offers parking and use of its boat ramp for a fee. An alternative launch site is the sewer pump station across the river downstream from the bridge; there is parking for one or two cars here.

35A RIVERHURST DRIVE/OSSIPEE ROAD (CO mile 7.2)
USGS Billerica quadrangle
The town of Billerica owns a small beach where these roads meet near the river, offering flat, easy access to the water. Several cars can park at the edge of the road.

36 OLD MIDDLESEX TURNPIKE, Billerica (CO mile 8.0)
USGS Billerica quadrangle
Downstream from the present Route 3, the Old Middlesex Turnpike crossed the Concord. Of its bridge, only the stone abutments remain. The old turnpike is now a narrow, dirt lane, blocked off at the road in recent years due to problems with illegal dumping. Brush along the road makes parking difficult.

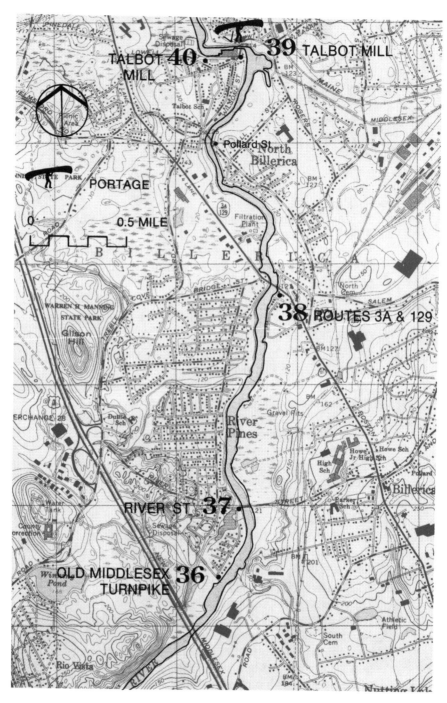

USGS 7.5': Billerica

Concord River: Town of Billerica

36 OLD MIDDLESEX TURNPIKE, Billerica (CO mile 8.0)
USGS Billerica quadrangle
Downstream from the present Route 3, the Old
Middlesex Turnpike crossed the Concord. Of its bridge,
only the stone abutments remain. The old turnpike is
now a narrow, dirt lane, blocked off at the road in recent
years due to problems with illegal dumping. Brush along
the road makes parking difficult.

37 RIVER STREET, Billerica (CO mile 8.4)
USGS Billerica quadrangle
At the left, upstream side of this bridge there is a river
access and along-the-road parking for a few cars.

38 ROUTES 3A and 129, Billerica (CO mile 9.5)
USGS Billerica quadrangle
A launch site with parking is available at Contribution Park,
on the right bank downstream from the bridge.
There is also access a short distance upstream from the
bridge, with parking in a commercial lot nearby.

39 TALBOT MILL (upstream access), Billerica
(CO mile 11.2)
USGS Billerica quadrangle
The river is reached from the parking lot on the left bank,
just upstream from the Lowell Street Dam.

40 TALBOT MILL (downstream access), (CO mile 11.2)
USGS Billerica quadrangle
Downstream from the large mill buildings the river runs
alongside a parking lot on the left bank.

Comments

The Concord River is a notable large-mouth bass fishery,
producing some trophy-sized fish every year. The Carlisle-
Bedford bridge (Access 34) is the midpoint of the section
most esteemed for bass fishing.

In Thoreau's time the Carlisle Road bridge was supported
by twenty wooden piers. It had been constructed by the two
towns it connected. Bedford built out from the east side, and
Carlisle from the west. There was a dispute about its location.
Carlisle succeeded in locating the bridge where there was high
ground on its side. Because the opposite shore is marshy,
Bedford had to build a long causeway.

This stretch of the river is broad enough and deep

93

enough to encourage motorboats, even water-skiing. The open water is 100 to 130 yards wide. On the left is a wide marsh; on the right are red maples. For a mile and a half, the river is far from roads and houses. The marshy left bank is an undeveloped part of Carlisle, the right bank, a forested section of Bedford. Billerica begins at Mill Brook (CO mile 5.5).

The marina just above the Route 4 bridge, (CO mile 6.6) allows parking and the use of their launch site for a fee. Across the river, downstream from the bridge, is a sewer pump station where an alternative launch site is available.

At CO mile 7.1, a small island is reached, a knob of bedrock. This island marks the northern extremity of one phase of an ancient lake (See page 103). The glacial lake was formed by ice that dammed the valley between these slopes, preventing the Concord River's passage to the north. The stone is Andover granite. Beyond the island, a high, steep bank is on the left. This high ridge is one of the most scenic points on the river. A lower hill is on the right. The rocky island and much of the land on both banks here is owned by Sudbury Valley Trustees and the Town of Billerica.

Below Route 3 (CO mile 7.7) several rocks are in the middle of the river, but they are easily avoided. Abutments that support the Old Middlesex Turnpike bridge (CO mile 8.0) are visible on both banks. The left bank is Access 36.

For the next mile, the right bank is marshy and undeveloped, but the left bank has many houses, which become flooded at high water.

At Routes 3A & 129 (CO mile 9.5) access is on the right, upstream from the bridge or at Contribution Park, downstream from the bridge.

Suggested Outings
— Downstream through this section.
Distance: 5.0 miles
Portages: None
Parking:
    Upstream — Bedford Boat Ramp, Access 34
    Downstream — Contribution Park or commercial lot near
                Routes 3A and 129, Access 38.
Note: This section may be canoed back and forth by paddling upstream from Routes 3A and 129. For beginners, this is a good place to get acquainted with handling a canoe. The broad, flat river will offer no difficulties unless the weather is windy. Most motorboats reduce speed when near canoes, thus moderating their wakes.

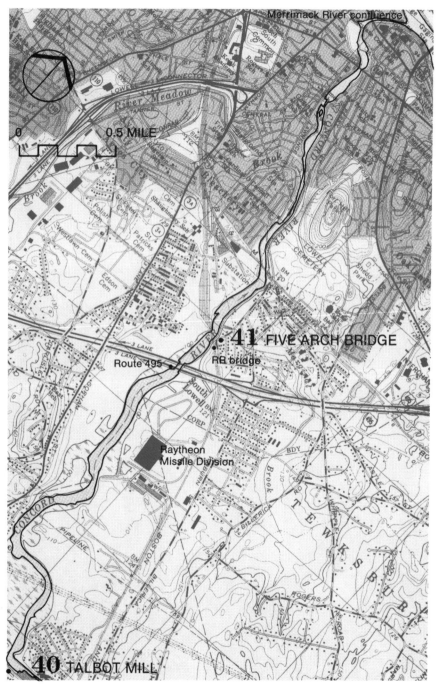

USGS 7.5': Billerica, Lowell

Concord River: Towns of Billerica, Chelmsford, Tewksbury; City of Lowell

Billerica, Lowell

Access Points

38 ROUTES 3A and 129, Billerica (CO mile 9.5) [See map page 92]
USGS Billerica quadrangle
A launch site with parking is available at Contribution Park, on the right bank downstream from the bridge.
There is also access a short distance upstream from the bridge, with parking in a commercial lot nearby.

39 TALBOT MILL (upstream access), Billerica (CO mile 11.2)
USGS Billerica quadrangle
The river is reached from the parking lot on the left bank, just upstream from the Lowell Street Dam.

40 TALBOT MILL (downstream access), (CO mile 11.2)
USGS Billerica quadrangle
Downstream from the large mill buildings the river runs alongside a parking lot on the left bank.

41 FIVE ARCH BRIDGE, Lowell (CO mile 13.3)
USGS Billerica quadrangle
On the right bank, just below the railroad bridge, Denton and Billerica Streets form a right angle near the river. Limited on-street parking is available.

Comments

The rocks and bridges of this part of the Concord don't lend themselves to motorboats, but they are no problem to canoeists.

The Billerica water filtration plant (CO mile 9.9) is on the left. Beyond Pollard Street (CO mile 10.4), the riverbed is littered with stone. This is the Fordway Bar.

The resistant rock of this formation of granodiorite has slowed the fall of the Concord for untold ages. In 1711, the first dam was built for a mill where the river tumbled off the northern end of the formation. The eleven-foot drop is the first substantial fall below Saxonville (northeast Framingham) on the Sudbury, or below West Concord on the Assabet.

In the early 1800s, the Middlesex Canal entered on the right bank (CO mile 10.8) through what is now a weed-choked backwater. See page 111 for the history of the canal. The bell in the Talbot Mills tower was used to call workers to the mill.

Take out at the parking lot (CO mile 11.0), which is on the left above the dam. Carry around the mill buildings, passing to their left. The downstream access point is in another parking lot.

The Concord resumes its flow between wooded banks and scattered boulders. Raytheon's Missile Systems Division (CO mile 12.6) looms on the right. A short distance beyond is the point at which Tewksbury, Billerica, Lowell, and Chelmsford come together, not in a precise point, but nearly so. Interstate 495 is just beyond (CO mile 13.1) followed by the five-arched railroad bridge. The final access point is past the bridge, on the right bank. It is possible to canoe safely to the next railroad bridge, but beyond that point the current can be strong. The river spills over a zigzag dam just below the Lawrence Street bridge (CO mile 13.9).

In Lowell, the Concord descends rapidly through a narrow valley. It is not recommended for canoeists. There are many obstructions, both natural and man-made, and few choices of channels. At some points necessary portages are difficult or impossible. The current is very strong.

The Talbot Mill in Billerica stands near the route of the Middlesex Canal.

Though unfit for canoeing, the lower two miles of the Concord are easily reached on foot and worth seeing. A utility access road is open to pedestrians along the right bank below Lawrence Street. It offers a good view of the zigzag dam and of the big mill building on the opposite bank. This mill tapped the Concord's water power prior to the harnessing of the Merrimack. Downstream there are several picturesque rapids and falls.

The mouth of the Concord can be viewed from behind St. John's Hospital in innermost urban Lowell. The Merrimack drinks the Concord in a gulp, and takes her to the ocean.

Suggested Outings
— From Talbot Mill, upstream and back.
Distance: Variable
Portages: None
Parking: In parking lot at mill.

— Downstream run of this section.
Distance: 3.8 miles
Portages: One, around Talbot Mill
Parking:
    Upstream — Contribution Park or commercial lot near Routes 3A and 129, Access 38.
    Downstream — On street near Five Arch Bridge, Access 41.

Part Two: History

Geology

Rivers flow past us at a rate both observable and comprehensible. The stone of Earth's crust also flows, but the velocity of its movement is so much slower than our lives that it is common sense to regard bedrock as permanent. Geologists, who have a different kind of common sense, think of time in such lanky stretches that "permanence" has no meaning. In geological time there are young rocks, old rocks, recycled rocks, generations of rocks. Geological concepts are at such odds with the world of our experience that they require a leap of scientific faith or imagination.

Based on the age of the oldest rocks brought back from the moon, scientists estimate that Earth is 4.6 billion years old. If a mountain two miles high erodes at the rate of one-hundredth of an inch per year, it is gone in only 12.7 million years. In 4.6 billion years, intervals of 12.7 million years are repeated 363 times. Earth's history spans so many millions of years that its crust has had time to pass through many generations. Eroded particles are carried downhill by wind and water. They accumulate at the bottom of the sea. They pile upon each other until the heat and pressure caused by the weight overhead changes the minerals from sediment to fresh stone. As huge stone masses collide, new mountains are displaced skyward. Our planet is geologically alive. Energy cycles through Earth and changes its rock faces and its cloud covers. Cloud movements are perceptible to us because they are so much faster. The clouds are part of a water cycle powered by solar energy. Rocks are in a slower cycle, powered by Earth's internal heat.

New England Bedrock
At Saxonville in Framingham, the Sudbury River plunges over a dam onto a mass of jet-black stone. How old is this stone? How was it formed? Of what minerals is it made? The answers to these questions lie in the field of "bedrock"

geology. This science deals in time that rolls backward in million-year units, back to the point 570 million years ago at which even geologists lose track of the generations of stone.

Roughly 400 million years ago, North America was on a collision course with Europe, creeping through a doomed ocean named Iapetus. Somewhere in that ocean lay chunks of continental rock, big islands, destined to become New England. Geologists call these the Gander and Avalonian Terranes. It is not clear where they came from, only that they were plastered onto the North American margin prior to its union with Europe. When the continents collided, great mountains crumpled skyward, and molten material from the mantle forced its way upward into cooler strata. The surface bedrock today is a complex collage of granite and basalt that resulted from these injections, plus the rock that underlay the Gander and Avalonian Terranes.

North America detached from Europe after some crustal stretching that created rift valleys such as the Connecticut River Valley. The Atlantic Ocean opened. The great mountains eroded and washed onto the continental shelf. The roots of the old mountains, including ancient sedimentary rocks from the terranes, plus granite and other igneous rock formed miles below, have risen to become the bedrock surface of today.

Like New England's life forms, its economy, and even its demography, the bedrock geology of New England is not a thing of grand sweeps, but a patchwork of intricate variety. Geologists describe continents as plates of less dense rock "floating" on the denser crustal rock of the sea floors. Patches of continent have spent eons migrating here and there on the earth's surface, driven, it is thought, by convection currents flowing in slow motion through rock which is so hot and under so much pressure that it is doughy. Convection currents are easily seen in a pot of water being heated on a stove; it is heat that powers them, just as heat from the earth's mantle pushes the continental plates.

One of the rocks underlying the Concord Basin is Dedham granite or granodiorite, an igneous rock formed from molten rock that cooled slowly while deep below the surface. Its colors include white, gray, pink and green in varying proportions. The colors appear in speckles about one-eighth of an inch across. You may find pebbles of this rock along the shore, but exposures of Dedham granite bedrock are harder to find.

Glacial Deposits

When we canoe the rivers, bedrock ledges such as those
visible at Saxonville on the Sudbury, or on the Assabet in
Maynard, or on the Concord in Lowell, are encountered
much less often than silt, sand, gravel, cobbles, and
boulders, which are the rotten remnants of bedrock. We find
such loose geological debris where it was left by glaciers
and their meltwater. It is ice that gave the Concord basin its
present form, relieving high places of soil and whatever
ledge was weathered enough to split off. The ice is thought
to have done its work over the past million years. The last
glacial ice sheet melted from the Concord Basin a mere
11,000 years ago: a miniscule fraction of Earth's history.

New England bedrock lies beneath a thin layer of
broken and powdered rock left when the ice sheet melted.
A little fresh soil has been produced in the short time since
glaciation, from decomposing stone and decaying vegetation.
Soil is thinnest on ridges and hillsides, where it varies from
inches to a few feet in depth. It becomes deeper along the
bases of the hills and in the valleys.

In some places glacial debris is piled high. Oval hills
called drumlins are scattered throughout the Concord
Basin. Orchard Hill (AS mile 17.0), at the Stow-Hudson
boundary, is an example. The gentle form of this drumlin is
all the more observable because it has been kept in grass.
At the top of Orchard Hill, not visible from the river, is a
"meltwater channel" washed out when ice melted from the
glacier that once lay overhead.

Today the Assabet winds around the north of Orchard
Hill. It is thought that prior to the Ice Age the Assabet ran
to the south of the hill, through the current locations of
Lake Boon and White's Pond, to merge with the Sudbury
near Heard Pond (SU mile 18.1). This change of course was
caused by the sudden drainage of a glacial lake.

Glacial lakes formed in the Concord Basin because the
flow of water was blocked by the slowly retreating glacial
ice. The bedrock slopes to the north, but meltwater could
not flow in that direction, so it filled the valleys until it over-
flowed into nearby basins: those of the east-flowing Charles
and the south-flowing Blackstone. The elevations of the
passes set the high-water position for the glacial lakes. Two
lakes dominated the valley: Glacial Lake Assabet, to the
west, and Glacial Lake Sudbury, to the east. The prolonged
deposition of sediment at the bottom of the glacial lake

accounts for the fertile, board-flat marsh and meadow that characterize the Sudbury Valley below Saxonville (SU mile 14.6) and in the vicinity of Concord village. The uppermost portions of the Sudbury Valley, Cedar Swamp and its environs, were at the bottom of Glacial Lake Assabet.

Glacial Lake Assabet curled around Orchard Hill, held from its former course by deposits of glacial debris and by ice dams. The channel to the north and east of Orchard Hill was carved because an ice dam melted there first. Water rushing out of the lake carried everything but bedrock from Gleasondale, originally named Rock Bottom for this reason. The torrent filled the valley to the east, squeezed between high hills into Maynard, and left that town with a stony gorge that offers white-water learners local training at times of high water.

When they melted, glaciers released their mineral burden into meltwater. The water dropped this material wherever the current stopped moving fast enough to carry it. Boulders fell where they were at melt-out. Gravel was carried along for a distance, sand farther, and clay didn't settle out until it reached a lake. A bewildering variety of earthforms with colorful names resulted from this process: drumlins, eskers, kames, sand plains, and fans. Glacial erratics, the huge boulders carried away from their natal bedrock, stand as monuments to the age of ice.

River Gradients
The profile of a river's bed determines how fast it flows. The angle of this incline, the gradient, is far too small to measure in degrees. It is expressed in feet per mile: feet of vertical fall per mile of horizontal river.

The Assabet descends 175 feet between the Nichols Dam in Westborough, and Egg Rock in Concord, an average of five and a half feet per mile. The Sudbury begins 20 feet lower than the Assabet, so its overall gradient is slightly less: five feet per mile. The Concord's average gradient is four and a half feet per mile. These averages do not indicate angry rivers. The truth is tamer still. The Sudbury does nearly all of its falling in its first sixteen miles. The lower half is nearly level. Between Heard Pond and Egg Rock the Sudbury drops a matter of inches. At flood stage, water pouring from the Assabet causes the Sudbury to flow backward. The Concord has a very slight gradient until it reaches Fordway Bar in North Billerica, a few miles above its mouth. Most of the Concord's fall is during its tumultuous passage through Lowell.

Energy from falling water is available in practical amounts at places where rivers drop rapidly. Sharp grades occur where bedrock has resisted erosion more stubbornly than rock just downstream, or where a fault has created a slope. In the Concord Basin, immigrating Europeans promptly used the water in such places to power mills to replace muscle power in the monotonous tasks of sawing wood, grinding grain, and pumping bellows.

Prehistory

During the 10,000 years between the retreat of the glaciers and the arrival of the Europeans, the Concord Basin was inhabited by peoples whose lives were closely tied to their environment. Until the present millenium they had no agriculture. All of these peoples are called Indians, but their cultures differed over time, in response to the changes in climate and resources.

Immediately after glacial retreat, the basin's climate and vegetation resembled those currently found in the subarctic. Although the cold must have challenged ancient humanity's survival abilities, the population of giant mammals sustained them. Mammoth, mastodon, giant beaver, bison, and caribou ranged over the landscape, which was, at first, barren of trees.

During the Ice Age, so much of the planet's water froze in continental glaciers that sea level fell. Nantucket, Martha's Vineyard, and Boston Harbor were surrounded by dry land. Mammoths grazed on George's Bank. Alaska could be reached on foot from Asia. Nomadic hunters from Siberia, wandering eastward, crossed to America. By 9,000 years ago people had spread throughout North and South America. These ancients, called Paleo-Indians, hunted the giant mammals with deadly efficiency. The massive herbivores had no experience with the aggressive carnivorous primates, our own species, recently arrived from the Old World.

As the supply of big game dwindled, and the climate warmed, the Paleo-Indian culture was superceded by a new way of life recognized by the artifacts it left behind. This is called the Archaic Period, and began 7,000 years ago. People used a wide variety of food sources, living in a style labelled "hunter-gatherer." Elk, deer, bear, and other animals were sought by Archaic-Indians. They gathered seeds, roots, berries, and nuts. To animals wary enough to have survived the Paleo-Indians, the odor, sight, and sound of humans must have inspired abject terror. Trapping became an increasingly preferable method of hunting, as it became difficult to approach within spear range of prey animals.

Judging by the plants that thrived here during the Archaic Period, scientists believe that the climate became warmer than it is today. The first post-glacial forest, of spruce and fir, gave way to hickory, oak, and pine. The middle of the Archaic Period was the golden age of hickories. It was also the time in which the Concord Basin was most heavily populated, prior to the arrival of the European colonists. From their examinations of sites such as the Flagg Swamp Rock Shelter, archaeologists know that hickory nuts, rich in calories, were part of the diet of the Archaic-Indians who lived in the basin.

At AS mile 8.8, in Marlborough, the Assabet passes under Interstate 290. During planning for the highway, an archaeological survey was made. The preliminary assessment indicated intensive prehistoric occupation of the space under an overhanging rock ledge. This rock shelter overlooked, and was named after, Flagg Swamp. A thorough investigation was made by a group of archaeologists from Harvard's Peabody Museum during the summer of 1980, prior to destruction of the site during highway construction.

The team concluded that the rock shelter had been used by family groups as a winter shelter from 4000 to 1000 years ago. Remains of the following items were found in quantities that imply that they were deliberately collected and consumed: hickorynuts and hazelnuts, acorns, freshwater clams, land snails, spotted and painted turtles, turkeys, heath hens, tomcod and alewives (plus the odd perch and trout), deer, elk, beaver, muskrat, and black bear.

Through investigations such as that at the Flagg Swamp Rock Shelter, archaeologists construct images of the lives of Archaic and Paleo Indians. Such images can only be assembled from undisturbed sites that have been systematically excavated. Individuals searching for curiosities to collect can permanently destroy the scientific value of a site. Those wishing to add to our knowledge of ancient man are encouraged to join the Massachusetts Archaeological Society (See Appendix 3) and to participate in digs supervised by professionals who have authorization from local historical commissions.

Agriculture came to Massachusetts about one thousand years ago, inaugurating the "Late Woodland" period. Woodland Indians created a mode of existence that added corn, beans, and squash to the Flagg Swamp menu. On the basis of the declining incidence of artifacts in the area dated to this time period, it appears that the Concord Basin was less populous than it had been. No doubt the people gathered at Saxonville Falls when the ocean-going fish swam upstream to spawn, and it is presumed that the river meadows grew some Indian crops. But on the whole, the Late Woodland population clung to the seaboard. The availability of clams and lobsters may have combined with a longer growing season to make the coastal region more attractive to the Indian farmers.

Woodland Indians in southern New England built dugout canoes from logs of pine, oak, or chestnut. They lit fires on the flattened upper surface of the log, scraped off the charred wood, and fired it again. The process was repeated until the log had been shaped into a canoe. Such vessels were durable and practical for the deep water of the Concord and lower Sudbury, but too heavy for portages.

Bark canoes were much lighter. The finest bark canoes were made in northern New England, near habitat suited to the growth of large white birch trees. In central New England, the bark of smaller birches was patched together into small canoes that could carry Indian hunters on forays to the headwaters.

The Woodland Period ended unhappily for the native Americans. Epidemics accompanied the arrival of the Europeans, reducing the native population so severely that the newcomers had little trouble shouldering aside the remaining population. When the English arrived, four Eastern Algonquian-speaking tribes lived in what became Massachusetts: the Nipmuck, Pawtucket, Massachusett, and Wampanoag. It is thought that their dialects were mutually intelligible. The tribes did not have a unifying political structure, but were divided into "sachemdoms."

Tribal Distribution
in Southern New England, 1630

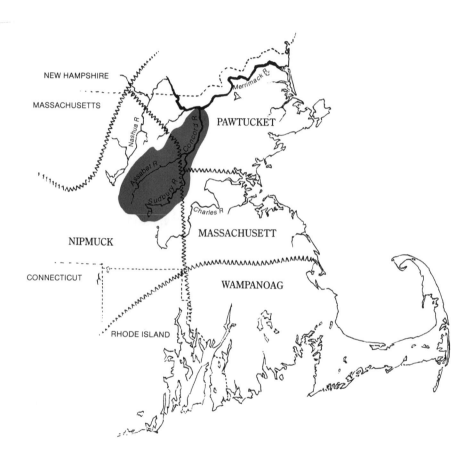

Although the leadership position of sachem was heredi-
tary, subjects could transfer their loyalty to other
sachems, so the wealth and power of a sachem was tied to
popularity.

The Concord Basin lies in the broad boundary between the Nipmuck, Pawtucket, and Massachusett tribal
areas. The lack of a controlling native political structure,
the gradual increase in trade with seafarers and resulting
epidemics, and the sudden impact of the flood of English
arrivals combine to obscure our view of the final stage of
indigenous Woodland culture in Massachusetts. We know
the diet of the Woodland Indians was varied. They lived
in structures framed with bent saplings and covered with
sheets of bark or woven mats. Using fire they kept the
forests clear of underbrush. They were sophisticated in
their medical knowledge. They welcomed the white newcomers with a guileless generosity that dissipated in the
years leading up to King Philip's War in 1676.

On the rivers of the Concord valley the canoeist is
never far from sites occupied by ancient people. We can
imagine the big-game-hunting Paleo-Indians ambushing a
mammoth along a trail to Cedar Swamp Pond, the huge
creature reeling before the onslaught of the spear-hurlers
as they spring from the cover of glacial boulders. We can
picture Archaic women gathering wild rice and other
seeds from river meadows, perhaps beating the grains
from their stalks into a canoe. Nearby, children splash in
the shallows, half-playing, half-working as they uproot
starchy tubers of yellow pond lilies and cattails, the sun
hot on their shoulders, but their feet cool in knee-deep
mud.

Part way up the hillside are the wigwams, fourteen
feet in diameter, positioned to catch insect-discouraging
breezes. Seated before the wigwam, a master of stone
craft works a chunk of stone obtained by trade from the
Blue Hills. He is making a knife by chipping off flakes
with rapid pecks of a hammer-stone. As he works, he tells
a story, entertaining grandchildren sprawled nearby. The
story features a powerful bear, terrible to the children.
The old man himself is quietly fearful of raiders from the
west. He occasionally looks up from his work to take a
searching glance in that direction.

In springtime, people congregate at the falls. The concentrations of fish allow them to be shoulder-to-shoulder

with other families for a time, and still find food. There are warm reunions and, perhaps, stiff encounters between teenagers newly come of age. To the Indians, the sound of rushing water must have evoked memories of springtime, courtship, and flirtation. The Calvinists were to hear, in the same sound, the power to turn machinery.

Settlement, Industry and Transportation

The Puritans established Boston and Watertown in 1630. Prime farmland in the Charles River Basin was quickly taken up, and settlers looked westward for more. The flat, treeless margin of the Concord, fertile with silt from Glacial Lake Sudbury, was a ready-made hayfield. Hay was needed to fuel draft animals, and to provide fodder for cattle, so farmers were attracted to the meadows. The towns of Concord and Billerica were established in 1635, and Sudbury in 1639. These towns originally included the preponderance of land in the entire Concord valley, subsequently divided into smaller towns through grants and petitions. Parent towns fought these divisions, fearing the loss of revenue, but outlying villages succeeded in gaining independence. Concord relinquished Acton and Carlisle. Sudbury gave up Wayland and Marlborough. Marlborough was further divided into Northborough, Westborough, Southborough, and Hudson.

Throughout the valley, the wet meadows were left for hay, and drier land was put to the plow. The resulting grain needed milling, so gristmills were constructed, not only on the rivers, but on many of the tributary brooks. Waterpower turned the stones that reduced the grain to flour. Waterpower converted logs to lumber in sawmills. Early mills were sometimes fitted with saws *and* stones, as was Savil Simpson's mill on the Sudbury in Ashland, built in 1706.

The Sudbury River had more than a dozen small- and medium-sized mills above Saxonville. Ashland alone had six. The site of the easternmost, the Cutler Mill, is now at the bottom of the Metropolitan District Commission's Reservoir #2. Ashland's mills ground grain, cut lumber, rolled paper, spun and wove fibers, and pumped a forge bellows.

Water was also used to power fulling mills. Fulling is a process for finishing handwoven cloth. At the fulling mill, cloth was washed in soapy water. Then it was impregnated with fuller's earth, a clay that absorbs lanolin. Waterpower was used to subject the cloth to prolonged pounding, after which the fuller's earth was removed by washing.

Before the use of steam engines, the potential production of a mill was limited by the amount of power at the site. Waterpower depends on the volume of water and the length of its drop. The largest mills were built where the greatest power was available. The most substantial mills on the Assabet were at Northborough, Hudson, Gleasondale (in Stow), Maynard, and Damondale (West Concord). The Sudbury's big mill was at Saxonville. The Concord powered a large complex in North Billerica, and another in Lowell. All of these mills were brick buildings, most still standing, characteristic of the streamside industrial architecture of New England.

These large mills extracted the power of the falling water with turbines, which are more efficient than water wheels. In a turbine, water falls down through a cylinder. Inside the cylinder are a series of blades, somewhat like the blades of a fan, which the water rotates as it passes downward. The rotary motion is carried to machinery through a series of axles, gears, or belts. Turbines began to replace water wheels in the 1820s.

A dam at North Billerica stored Concord River water for another use. The Middlesex Canal provided water transportation from the Merrimack River to Boston, beginning in 1803. An incidental effect was that boats could travel from Sudbury and Concord to Charlestown and Boston. In 1815, passenger service was offered on Mondays, Wednesdays, and Fridays. Passengers boarded a horse-drawn gondola at the canal's Lowell terminus. The twenty-seven-mile trip began at 8:00 A.M. and delivered passengers to Charlestown at 2:00 P.M. The fare was seventy-five cents. The route passed through Chelmsford, Billerica, Wilmington, Woburn, Winchester, Medford, and Somerville before reaching the Mystic River and Charlestown. In Wilmington the canal crossed over the Shawsheen River by way of an aqueduct.

The entire canal floated boats on water from the Concord River, because the Concord at North Billerica was higher than the canal's outlets at the Merrimack and the Mystic. Water was let down in each direction from North Billerica through a series of twenty locks.

For efficient movement of passengers and freight, the Middlesex Canal had one chief drawback: ice closed it in the winter. A new method of land transportation could operate in all seasons. The Boston and Worcester Railroad linked those cities in 1835. Businessmen in Boston were boosters of this railroad because they wanted access to products carried on the Erie Canal, which connected the Hudson River to the nation's new granary in the Ohio valley. Until Boston's railroad extended to Albany, goods from the Erie Canal had to pass through New York City before reaching Boston or other seaboard cities. The Boston and Worcester linked with the Western Railroad to Springfield in 1839, and reached the Hudson at Albany in 1841. Today this rail line follows nearly its original route as it passes along the Sudbury in Ashland, Southborough, Hopkinton, and Westborough. At Assabet Reservoir it crosses the headwaters of the Assabet. It is the busiest railroad in New England, and one of the busiest in the country.

Rail service also opened to Lowell in the same season it opened to Worcester, the summer of 1835. Railroad competition diminished the need for the Middlesex Canal, which ceased operations in the 1840s. But the North Billerica dam continued in use, supplying water to the growing mills.

The owners of river meadows in Concord, Sudbury, and Wayland complained that the Billerica dam raised the level of the river enough to ruin the meadows for growing hay. The Massachusetts trend toward industry and away from agriculture was not changed by their complaints.

The mill interests were themselves threatened by an even greater political power. In 1848, Boston began taking drinking water from Long Pond, now known as Lake Cochituate. This water had been an important source of the Sudbury, and its loss threatened mill operations. To avoid a lawsuit, the City of Boston built Fort Meadow Reservoir, in the Marlborough-Hudson area, and Lake Whitehall in Hopkinton. The purpose of these reservoirs was to store water during wet periods. By releasing this water when the river was low, a minimum flow could be maintained, and the mills would not miss the Long Pond Water.

The respite was temporary. After 1878, much of the upper Sudbury River was shunted to Chestnut Hill Reservoir for Boston's use. This diversion was reduced when water from the Wachusett Reservoir entered the system in 1898. Since Quabbin Reservoir went into service in the 1940s, the Sudbury reservoirs have not been used, but have been maintained as a backup supply. Resumption of the diversion is contemplated.

The taking of upper Sudbury water for drinking caused interest in its cleanliness. The lower Sudbury, the Concord, and especially the Assabet lacked this consideration. Early industrial users disregarded the effect of their actions on water quality. The *amount* of water was important to downstream interests, but in the ethics of the age rivers were used to carry off whatever would wash away. The resulting damage is still being mended.

Water Quality

In 1900, the Massachusetts Board of Health investigated the Concord Basin rivers. It had been charged to do so by a resolution of the legislature that mentioned industrial discharges:

> At Saxonville a considerable quantity of water polluted in the processes of scouring wool and washing cloth (renders the Sudbury) very foul for a long distance below the village.

The Board of Health issued its report the following year, stating that the most significant sources of pollution were to the Assabet River at Northborough, Hudson, Stow, Maynard, Acton, and Concord. At Northborough:

> The sewage of about 400 mill operatives is discharged directly into the stream; and the spent dyes and 5000 gallons per day of water used for washing cloth from the Northboro Woolen Company.

> In Hudson the river receives the sewage from 18 business blocks including three hotels, 22,000 gallons per day of wool-scouring waste, 30,000 gallons per day of water used for washing hides in which process soap, lime water, and tan liquor are used; and the sewage from 700 employees in 3 shoe factories.

At Gleasondale the sewage from 85 employees, and 3000 gallons per day of waste.

At Maynard, the waste from scouring wool, and the sewage of 950 employees.

At Concord, sewage from 165 employees, and 110,000 gallons per day sewage from the Reformatory.

Mill closings did not stop exploitation of the rivers. As the pollution from mills lessened, the pollution from inadequate sewage treatment became much worse because of an increased population. Today the Assabet receives wastewater discharges at Westborough (from Westborough, Shrewsbury, and Hopkinton), Marlborough, Hudson, Maynard, and MCI Concord, and from eight licensed industries. The Sudbury receives discharges from Marlborough, via Hop Brook, and the Raytheon Corporation in Wayland. Concord, Billerica, and the Billerica House of Correction discharge wastewater into the Concord, as do three industries licensed to do so.

Because so much Assabet water is from wastewater treatment plants, the river suffers from any deficiency in treatment. Key plants have been upgraded in recent years. The effluent from the new plants must meet national clean water standards. But treatment does not eliminate surplus nutrients, compounds of nitrogen and phosphorous, that encourage too-abundant vegetation. Such pollutants also wash into the rivers from lawns and farms.

The people who make the quality of the Concord Basin rivers their daily business are employees of the Commonwealth of Massachusetts. They are environmental engineers and biologists in the Technical Services Branch of the Division of Water Pollution Control in the Department of Environmental Protection. Their office is in Westborough near the sources of the Sudbury and Assabet Rivers. People from the Technical Services Branch take samples of water at points along the rivers, test for the presence of various chemicals, record the results, and issue periodic reports.

The state now designates the Sudbury, Assabet, and Concord Rivers as Class B Inland Waters.

Waters assigned to this class are designated for the uses of protection and propagation of fish, other aquatic life and wildlife; and for primary and secondary contact recreation.

You can swim, fish, and boat in water that meets Class B specifications as to oxygen content, temperature, and bacteria levels. The Sudbury, Assabet, and Concord rivers usually, but not always, meet Class B requirements.

The Technical Services Branch periodically monitors the wholesomeness of river fish. Because fish are high on the food chain, toxic chemicals present in the river system become concentrated in their flesh. In 1986, such testing indicated unsafe levels of mercury in Sudbury River fish. The acceptable level of mercury is one part per million. Some Sudbury fish were found to contain up to twelve parts per million. As a result, the state posted signs warning people against eating fish from the Sudbury. Fish from the Concord and Assabet rivers were not found to be contaminated.

The contamination is not in the water itself, but in the sediments. Creatures that live in and on the bottom pick up the poison in minute quantities, and pass it up the food chain when they are eaten by larger animals. The source

of the mercury is the Nyanza site in Ashland (SU mile 6.3). This toxic-waste dump was created by a series of dye manufacturers and last owned by a company called Nyanza. The site is on America's "ten worst" list. It has been the subject of an extensive, expensive cleanup effort, but new sources of contamination have been discovered on the property, which is a few hundred yards south of the Sudbury, just beyond the railroad embankment.

In recent years, the water quality of the Concord, Sudbury, and Assabet rivers has improved because of the actions of various levels of government, of cooperating industries, and of conservation organizations. The Assabet is cleaner than it has been in a century. Only in the past decade has it made sense to explore the Assabet by canoe. Continued improvement depends on steady government enforcement of water-pollution controls and a concerned and vocal constituency for the rivers.

Naturalists of the Concord Basin

The philosopher Ralph Waldo Emerson took issue with those who viewed the natural world as an object of conquest and exploitation. He found it a source of spiritual sustenance. In 1836 Emerson published these paragraphs in *Nature:*

> The greatest delight which the fields and woods minister is the suggestion of an occult relation between man and the vegetable. I am not alone and unacknowledged. They nod to me, and I to them. The waving of the boughs in the storm is new to me and old. It takes me by surprise, and yet it is not unknown. Its effect is like that of a higher thought or a better emotion coming over me.

> Through all its kingdom, to the suburbs and outskirts of things, (nature) is faithful to the cause whence it had its origin. It always speaks of Spirit. It suggests the absolute. It is a perpetual effect. It is a great shadow pointing always to the sun behind us.

Henry David Thoreau was at Harvard when Emerson wrote *Nature.* For several years of his young manhood,

before his stay at Walden Pond, Thoreau lived in Emerson's home. Their lives and thoughts entwined, but their emphases were different. Emerson's interest in nature was abstract. Thoreau took a sensory approach.
From Thoreau's journal:

> *July 10, 1852 Assabet River*
> I wonder if any Roman emperor ever indulged in such luxury as this — of walking up and down a river in torrid weather with only a hat to shade the head. What were the baths of Caracalla to this? Now we traverse a long water plain some two feet deep; now we descend into a darker river valley, where the bottom is lost sight of and the water rises to our armpits; now we go over a hard iron pan; now we stoop and go under a low bough of the *Salix nigra*; now we slump into soft mud amid the pads of the *Nymphaea odorata*, at this hour shut.

None of Thoreau's successors have published accounts of themselves sloshing naked along our river margins.

From 1886 to 1917, William Brewster recorded the comings and goings of birds and other creatures in the Concord Basin. His journals were extensive, scientific, and readable. Portions were published after his death as *October Farm* and *Concord River*. Brewster reports observations and impressions. He rambles physically over the landscape, but does not, like Thoreau, ramble over the page.

The ornithologist Ludlow Griscom had an even more rigorous approach than Brewster. Griscom sought numbers, trends and causes. He availed himself of the notes and journals Brewster left to Harvard. Griscom gathered information from amateur naturalists. He spent much time in the field, and took along youngsters who shared his interest, such as Allen Morgan, subsequently a founder and executive director of the Sudbury Valley Trustees.

Referring to the Concord area, Griscom wrote the following in 1949:

> This section is a historic bit of eastern Massachusetts... It is definitely a rural area, and, barring the town and village centers and their immediate vicinity, no substantial increase in population has taken place in a century.
> *Birds of Concord*

He ought to have touched wood when he wrote that, for within a few years the population exploded. Farm and forest have been on the run ever since. Circumstances have forced Massachusetts' naturalists to go beyond exploring and interpreting the natural world. They have had to defend its very existence. Thoreau was a naturalist-philosopher. Brewster and Griscom were naturalist-scientists. Allen Morgan, whose field observations were frequently cited by Ludlow Griscom, is not primarily a scientist. His work, and that of Sudbury Valley Trustees, is conservation and education.

Why has this small region produced so many accomplished naturalists? Outdoor Massachusetts has an inviting charm, an intimacy of scale, that distinguishes its beauty from the magnificence of America's west, and from all places where nature unfolds by the hundred-mile, rather than by the yard. Massachusetts' nature is benign. It lacks scorpions, flash floods, and wild, endless forest fires. In our basin, an hour of walking can encompass marsh, swamp, stream, field, and hilltop. The gentleness and variety of this area may partly account for the extraordinary tradition of Concord Basin naturalists and writers that began with Ralph Waldo Emerson and continues in the present day. The words and thoughts of these people have reached far beyond the boundaries of their home valley to help humans understand and appreciate their connections with the natural world.

Part Three: Natural History

The field guides listed in Appendix 4 identify thousands of different life forms, the vast majority of which do not appear in our area. The natural history section of this book takes the opposite approach: few life forms are mentioned, but they *all* live in the Concord Basin for at least part of the year. The species chosen are those most readily observed by canoeists, plus some of special interest. They are native to this area except as indicated in the descriptions.

Plants

At many points on the upper Sudbury and Assabet, tree limbs form a ceiling above the rivers. At such places, plants completely surround the canoeist. Trees are overhead, aquatic vegetation is under the boat, and streamside plants stand in lush ranks on either hand. The diversity of plants at first overwhelms those of us untutored in botany. We react as humans always do when confronted with myriad unnamable forms: we tend not to notice them. We must learn some of their names before we can give plants their proper regard.

In the outdoors as well as at the dinner table, appreciation of vegetables increases with age. Plants struggle as we do to mature and to bear fruit, and in this we can recognize our kinship with them.

Trees

Red Maple (swamp maple)
Acer rubrum
Maple family
Two species of maples appear on our rivers: red and silver. Red maples have smaller, redder seeds, and sharp angles between the lobes of their leaves. Silver maple leaves have rounded angles and deep indentations between their lobes. The central lobe of a red maple leaf is widest at its base, whereas the central lobes of silver maple leaves flare from a narrow base.

Red maples flower in early spring before they leaf out. The flowers are red, and appear in stalkless clusters along the twigs. Male flowers are yellow-red; female flowers are bright scarlet. The fruit are in pairs. Each is about an inch long. These mature quickly and drop from the trees in June. They descend, whirling, to the river's surface.

Red maples form pure stands in swamps due to their unusual tolerance for prolonged seasonal flooding. On hillsides they mix with oaks, pines, and birches. Red maple wood is used for pulp, pallets, canoe paddles, and fuel. Its sap can be used for maple syrup, but the sugar content is lower than that of the sugar maple.

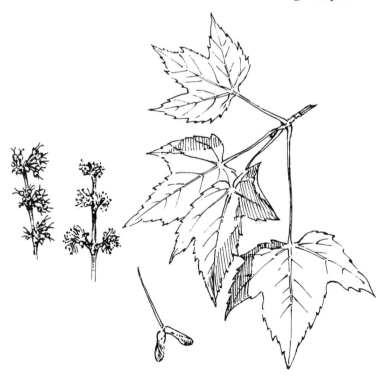

Silver Maple
Acer saccharinum
Maple family
Silver maples have greenish-yellow
male flowers and reddish female
flowers. Silver maple blooms earlier
than any other native New England
tree, and about two weeks before red
maple. The winged fruit is one and a
half to two and a half inches long. It
begins light green, but turns light
brown.

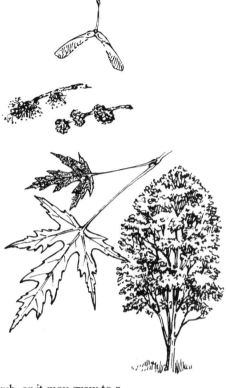

Silver maples are common along the
Assabet and Concord Rivers, and the
upper Sudbury. They grow rapidly, but
their branches are rather brittle and
break easily. When this happens over
the river the resulting obstacle is
called a "strainer;" water passes
through, but not your canoe. Silver
maples harvested in New England are
usually pulped for use in making
paper.

Black Willow (swamp willow)
Salix nigra
Willow family
Black willow may take the form of a shrub, or it may grow to a
sixty-foot tree. Plants in the willow family have separate male and
female individuals. Male flowers are yellowish catkins, female
catkins are whitish; both are erect. The
flowers appear in early spring with the
developing leaves.

Black willows grow beside our rivers
in many locations. Their roots help
hold the soil in place during floods,
reducing erosion. The wood of the
black willow is soft, light, and weak. It
was formerly made into charcoal for
the manufacture of gunpowder. Today
willow wood is used for baskets, pack-
ing material, and boxes.

River Birch
Betula nigra
Birch family
In the birch family, male catkins are long and pendulous, while female catkins are short and erect. The fruit is a small, hairy, two-winged nutlet that matures in late spring or early summer. The bark of river birch separates in papery scales. It is a shiny pinkish-brown or gray.

River birch is native to North America but not to Massachusetts; it was introduced from the southeastern United States. The wood is light, soft, and strong. It is used for wooden bowls, baskets, and furniture.

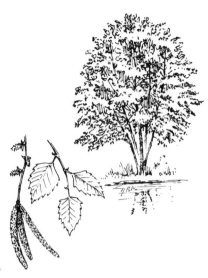

Hemlock
Tsuga canadensis
Pine family
Hemlock needles have two white stripes underneath. Hemlock cones are about three-fourths of an inch long, and hang from the tips of twigs. The cones mature in the fall, but usually remain on the tree until spring.

The feathery hemlock is the evergreen most likely to be seen at the water's edge. The tannin in hemlock bark was once used in making leather. Tea can be made from the twigs. Hemlock wood is considered difficult to work with because it tends to twist.

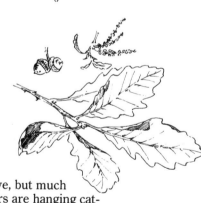

Swamp White Oak
Quercus bicolor
Beech family
Swamp white oak leaves are green above, but much lighter on their undersides. Male flowers are hanging catkins four to five inches long. Oak pollen creates a spring hayfever season for those sensitive to it. Female flowers occur singly or in small groups. The fruit is an acorn, of course. They grow on long stalks, usually in pairs.

The strong, heavy wood is used for furniture, cabinetry, flooring, and firewood.

Shrubs

Buttonbush
Cephalanthus occidentalis
Bedstraw family (Madder family)
Plant height: 3'-10'
Buttonbush is common along our rivers where there is full sun. It tolerates flooding but not shade. In late July or August spherical clusters of white flowers appear. Each flower is tiny, but the eye-catching cluster is one and a half inches in diameter.

Buttonbush is a preferred nesting site of green-backed herons and red-winged blackbirds. When dry, its fruit splits into small nutlets which are eaten by ducks.

Elderberry (common elder)
Sambucus canadensis
Honeysuckle family
Plant height: 3'- 12'
The bright white flowers of elderberry open in June. Each flower is only a sixth of an inch across, but the flat-topped clusters are two to ten inches in diameter. The twigs have large, white, spongy pith. The flower stalks turn purple while fruits are maturing. The compound leaves have as many as eleven leaflets, each two to five inches long.

Elderberries produce purple or black berry-like fruit that has a bitter taste, but is good for making elderberry wine and jelly. Elderberries ripen in late August. They are an important food source for many birds.

Highbush Blueberry
Vaccinium corymbosum
Heath family
Plant height: to 10′
This is the species adapted for commercial blueberry production. It occurs in its wild state on low, wet land throughout the Concord Basin, frequently at the river's edge. The flowers appear in May or June, pure white or tinged with pink, a quarter inch to a half inch in length.

The sweet blue-black fruit ripens in late July or August. Blueberries are an important food for birds and mammals.

Multiflora Rose
Rosa multiflora
Rose family
Plant height: 6′- 8′
Multiflora rose was introduced from Europe. Its many white flowers bloom in May or June. They are three-quarters of an inch to one-and-a-half inches in diameter.

The fruit, a dull red rose hip, is eaten by birds, and the seeds are thereby distributed. Multiflora rose forms impenetrable masses which provide excellent songbird nest sites. For a time it was promoted to farmers as a maintenance-free "living fence," but some complain that it takes over the pasture.

Arrowwood (smooth arrowwood, northern arrowwood)
Viburnum recognitum
Honeysuckle family
Plant height: 3'- 9'
Arrowwood is so named because Indians are said to have used its slender, straight shoots to make arrow shafts.

The white flowers of arrowwood bloom in June. Their flat-topped clusters might be confused with those of elderberry, but the leaves of arrowwood are simple, round, and much more coarsely serrated than elderberry leaflets. The small flowers are in clusters two to four inches wide. The blue or black berries mature in August.

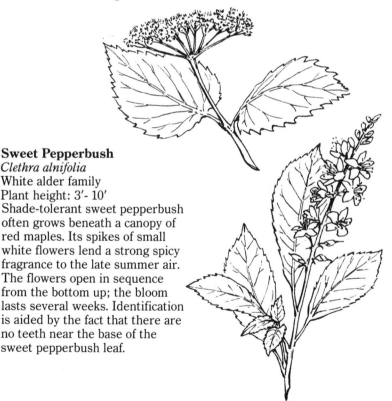

Sweet Pepperbush
Clethra alnifolia
White alder family
Plant height: 3'- 10'
Shade-tolerant sweet pepperbush often grows beneath a canopy of red maples. Its spikes of small white flowers lend a strong spicy fragrance to the late summer air. The flowers open in sequence from the bottom up; the bloom lasts several weeks. Identification is aided by the fact that there are no teeth near the base of the sweet pepperbush leaf.

Streamside Wildflowers

Yellow Flag (yellow iris, yellow sword flag)
Iris pseudacorus
Iris family
Plant height: to 3'
In June, the brilliant yellow blossoms appear between the long, stiff, sword-like leaves. Yellow flag is of European origin; it is said to have "escaped from cultivation" as if it had leaped over a garden wall and made a break for freedom. "Flag" is from the middle English *flagge,* which means "rush" or "reed." The banks of the Assabet between downtown Hudson and Stow boast a number of colonies of yellow flag.

Blue Flag
Iris versicolor
Iris famly
Plant height: 8" - 32"
This native iris has spectacular violet-blue flowers, purple veined, glowing with yellow at the base of their sepals. Sepal is the botanically correct name for what appear to be outer petals. The actual petals are narrower, and stand upright. Blue flag blooms in May or June. The pattern on the inner surface of the sepal serves to guide nectar-seeking insects into the chamber formed by the style and sepal, where they obtain their sweet reward, and inadvertently pollinate the flower.

The blue flag's rhizome is extremely poisonous, but was dried and used in small amounts as medicine by Indians and colonists.

Bittersweet Nightshade (nightshade, climbing nightshade)
Solanum dulcamara
Nightshade family
Vine length: 2' - 8 '
Bittersweet nightshade is a vine that finds its way to the streamside sunlight on shrubs. Although they span a mere half inch, the flowers are striking. The five stamens are fused into a bright yellow cone that contrasts with purple petals. Nightshade flowers continue to open from June to August. The fruit is an inedible berry an inch long, which ripens to red.

Bittersweet nightshade was introduced from Europe. It was used in England to counteract witchcraft.

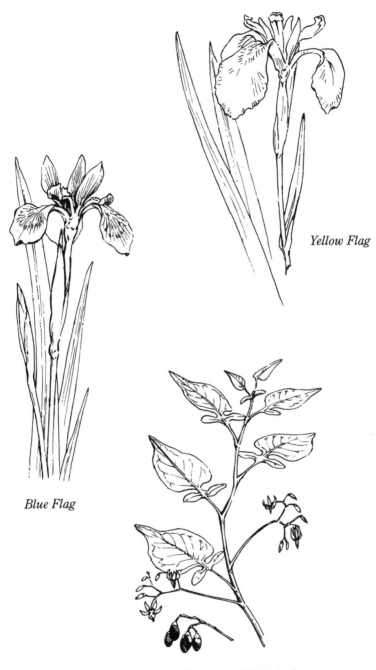

Yellow Flag

Blue Flag

Bittersweet Nightshade

129

Jewelweed (spotted touch-me-not)
Impatiens capensis
Touch-me-not family
Plant height: 2'- 5'
Jewelweed flowers are orange with reddish spots. Each scoop-shaped blossom is an inch long. The stems are smooth, translucent, and full of sap, which is used to reduce the itching of poison ivy and athlete's foot. When ripe, the fruit is spring loaded; it explodes when touched, and the seeds are catapulted from their capsules.

Jewelweed blooms from July to September, in full sun or partial shade. It is pollinated by bees, butterflies, and hummingbirds.

Purple Loosestrife
Lythrum salicaria
Loosestrife family
Plant height: 2'- 5'
Magenta spires of purple loosestrife appear in wet locations from July to September. Each flower is about half an inch in diameter. Flowers cover a spire that is six or more inches in length. The square stems of purple loosestrife are clasped by the bases of the leaves; each pair is at right angles to the pair above it.

Purple loosestrife has invaded the United States from Europe. It lends color to the landscape, but the enjoyment of naturalists is tempered by their awareness that purple loosestrife tends to crowd out native plants of greater value to ducks and other wildlife. Purple loosestrife is abundant along the Sudbury, forming magenta masses that arrest the eye of drivers crossing the river on Route 117.

Cardinal Flower
Lobelia cardinalis
Bluebell family
Plant height: 2'- 4'
Cardinal flower plants put out vivid scarlet blossoms at the top of their erect individual stalks. Each flower is one-and-a-half inches long; too long for the tongues of most insects to reach the nectar deep within the flower. Cardinal flower is pollinated chiefly by hummingbirds. The eyes of bees are not sensitive to red light, but hummingbirds are attracted to this color.

Cardinal flowers begin to open in late July; a few are still in bloom in September. They favor partially shaded streamside locations and vary in abundance from year to year.

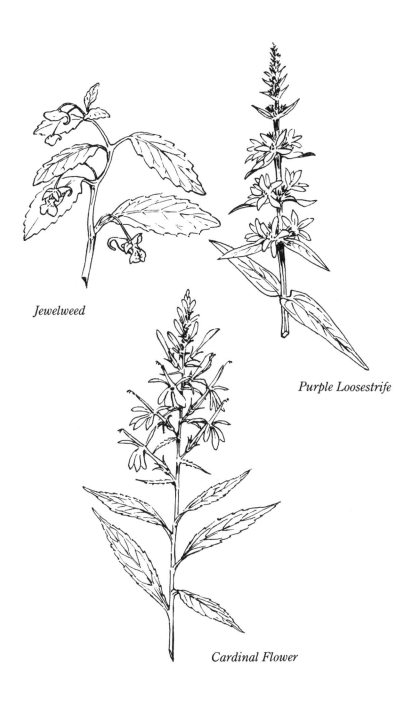

Jewelweed

Purple Loosestrife

Cardinal Flower

Swamp Smartweed
Polygonum coccineum and other species
Buckwheat family
Plant height: 2'- 3'
Each pink swamp smartweed flower is a sixth of an inch long; clusters vary between two and seven inches. Like most of the herbaceous plants found at or in the stream, swamp smartweed blooms late in the season, July to September, when the water level is lower and steadier than in the spring. Many of the forty-odd species in the genus *Polygonum* can be distinguished only by minor traits.

Swamp smartweed is very common along our rivers. It forms shoals in the channel through Cedar Swamp in the uppermost miles of the Sudbury. Its nutlets are eaten by ducks and other birds and by deer.

Sweetflag (calamus)
Acorus calamus
Arum family
Plant height: 1'- 4'
The yellow flowers of sweetflag occur on a stalk called a spadix, approximately three inches in length, on which tiny individual flowers are crowded together. A special leaf called a spathe projects a foot beyond the flower. Sweetflag blooms from May to July. Its long stiff leaves are aromatic, as is the rootstock, which formerly provided sweet-flavored material for candy and medicines. Muskrats love it.

Pickerelweed
Pontederia cordata
Pickerelweed family
Plant height: 1'- 2'
Pickerelweed is common along our riverbanks. Its violet flowers are a third of an inch wide and grow on spikes four inches in length. They bloom, in late summer. Their seeds can be eaten like nuts, and their young leafstalks can be cooked as greens. White-tailed deer consume pickerelweed.

Arrowhead
Sagittaria latifolia
Water plantain family
Plant height: 1'- 4'
Trios of white arrowhead flowers appear in late summer, each three quarters of an inch across. The lower flowers, which are female, usually open before the upper flowers, which are male. This facilitates cross-pollination. The female flowers produce small balls of seeds in whorls of three.

Submerged by the high water of spring, arrowhead puts out narrow, ribbonlike foliage that offers little resistance to the current and a large surface area for the exchange of oxygen and carbon dioxide. When the water level goes down, these leaves drop off and are replaced by new ones adapted for life above the water. These aerial leaves may be broad and rounded, narrow and linear, or any shape in between.

Beneath the mud, arrowhead produces edible starchy tubers eaten by ducks and muskrats and known as "duck potatoes." Ducks also eat the nutlets.

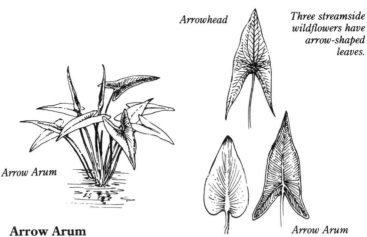

Arrowhead

Three streamside wildflowers have arrow-shaped leaves.

Arrow Arum

Arrow Arum

Pickerelweed

Arrow Arum
Peltandra virginica
Arum family
Plant height: 1'- 2'
The flower of arrow arum is within a spathe, which is a characteristic of the arum family. Arrow arum's spathe is green. The months of bloom are May to July. An oval ball of berries comes after the flowers.

Of the three plants with arrowhead-shaped leaves that are common in our river basin, the flowers of arrow arum are the least showy. Arrowhead has white flowers, those of pickerelweed are violet, and each is quite distinct in form. When not in bloom, these plants may be identified by the pattern of the veins in their leaves.

Joe-Pye Weed (spotted joe-pye weed)
Eupatorium maculatum and *E. dubium*
Aster family
Plant height: 3'- 6'
Joe-pye weed flowers appear between July and September in pinkish-purple clusters five inches in diameter. The stem is spotted or purple. Folklore reports that an Indian named Joe Pye used this plant to cure fevers.

Swamp Loosestrife (water willow, water oleander)
Decodon verticillatus
Loosestrife family
Plant height: to 6'
Whorls of deep pink blossoms open next to the stems in July and August. Swamp loosestrife stems are usually bent over, which is why the plant is often called water willow. These stems may be eight feet long. Where a stem tip touches the water, a spongy tissue may develop that can send out roots of its own. Using this tactic, swamp loosestrife invades open water. It abounds at Cedar Swamp Pond.

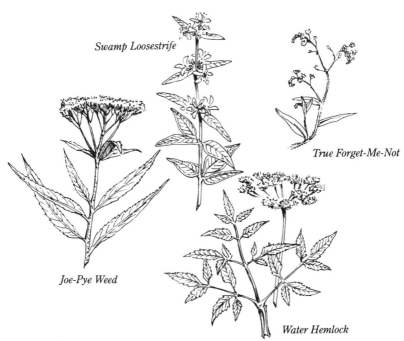

Swamp Loosestrife

True Forget-Me-Not

Joe-Pye Weed

Water Hemlock

True Forget-Me-Not
Myosotis scorpioides
Borage family
Plant height: 6"- 24"
The foliage of true forget-me-not forms bright green carpets,
often submerged, that retain their color into the cold months.
The tiny yellow-eyed blue flowers bloom from June to October,
in lush, cheerful masses. True forget-me-not is a native of
Europe. It is plentiful on the upper Sudbury in the
Southborough-Hopkinton area.

Water Hemlock (cowbane)
Cicuta maculata
Carrot family
Plant height: 2'- 6'
All parts of water hemlock are extremely poisonous; it was the
extract of the root of a close relative that killed Socrates. Small
white flowers form three-inch clusters above the leafy portion
of the plant. The months of bloom are July, August, and September. The stem is thick and smooth, often purplish or
streaked with purple. Another plant in the genus *Cicuta*, called
"bulb-bearing water hemlock," *C. bulbifera*, has long narrow
leaves. Both species occur in the Concord Basin.

Marsh Plants

Common Cattail (broad-leaved cattail)
Typha latifolia
Cattail family
Height: 3'- 7'
The spongy, cigar-shaped "cat's tail" is made up of female
flowers that have no petals. A narrow spike above it bears
yellowish male flowers, which fall off after yielding their pollen,
leaving the naked stalk. The leaves of common cattail are about
an inch wide. Narrow-leaved cattail, *Typha angustifolia,* also
occurs along our rivers. It is distinguished from common cattail
by its narrower leaves and by the space of a half inch between
the male and female flower spikes. Those on the common cattail
are usually contiguous.

Cattails are perennials that spread by creeping rootstocks. Often their leaves are covered with aphids. Both the leaves and the stems are mined by caterpillars and punctured by beetles. By supporting so many insects, cattails provide a rich food supply for birds. Marsh wrens and other wetland birds nest within dense stands of cattails. Its tubers are a favorite food of the muskrat. Cattails were used as food by Indians. The rootstock can be collected in fall or winter, dried, and ground into flour. Seeds and young stems can be eaten raw. The cat's tails are roasted.

Cattail plants have been shown to be highly efficient at removing pollutants, particularly surplus nutrients, from water.

Tussock Sedge
Carex stricta
Sedge family
Height: 3′

Tussock sedge is a common perennial that forms dense clumps in standing water, "tussocks" that are two to three feet high. The stems are rough and triangular. It flowers between July and September. The flowers are pollinated by wind, so they lack the bright colors other plants use to attract insects. The female flower clusters are narrow and reddish, and the male tan and shaggy.

The roots and sprouts of tussock sedge are eaten by muskrats. The seeds are eaten by ducks and other birds.

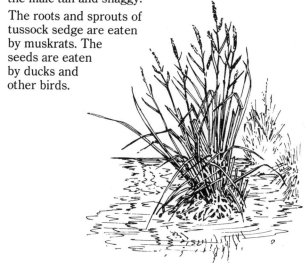

Great Bulrush
(soft-stem bulrush)
Scirpus validus
Sedge family
Height: 6'
Great bulrush grows in clumps. Its round stems are grayish-green and easily squashed. The reddish-brown flowers are in droopy cone-shaped clusters. Great bulrush is a valuable wildlife food; its shoots, nutlets, and tubers are eaten by ducks and geese. Great bulrush is a common native perennial.

Soft Rush (tufted rush)
Juncus effusus
Rush family
Height: 2'- 4'
Plants in the rush family have subdued flowers like those of grasses and sedges. The greenish flower clusters of soft rush turn brown as they mature in late summer. Soft rush grows in clumps, which provide shelter for birds. Muskrats feed on the rootstalks.

Wild Rice (water oats)
Zizania aquatica
Grass family
Height: 4'- 6'
The flowers of wild rice are bright yellow green. The branches stay after the flowers have fallen off. Female flowers are on the bristles of the plant's brush-like crown. The straw-colored or purplish male flowers droop from branchlets just below the crown.

This native annual is more widespread along our rivers than it was in previous centuries; it has been encouraged in order to attract and feed waterfowl. Fish also eat it.

138

Wild rice is related to white rice only by virtue of their both being in the grass family. Most wild rice sold in the United States comes from Minnesota. The long, narrow seeds fall off when touched, which makes it difficult to cultivate commercially.

Reed Canarygrass
Phalaris arundinacea
Grass family
Height: 3' - 4'
Reed canarygrass flowers early in the summer. Dried flowers remain above the leaves for the rest of the season. The hairiness of grass flowers aids them in catching grains of wind-born pollen. Reed canarygrass is a perennial that makes good hay. It grows naturally in wet lowland meadows. Such meadows at the fringes of Cedar Swamp were formerly harvested with horse-drawn equipment, but since the advent of heavier farm vehicles they have been allowed to grow up with shrubs and trees.

Burreed
Sparganium americanum
and similar species
Burreed family
Height: up to 3'
Burreed flowers throughout late spring and summer. The female flowers are packed into round, burr-like balls which are a half to one inch in diameter. The male flowers are also ball-shaped but are smaller. The ribbon-like leaves of burreed are often submerged, inviting confusion with the submerged form of arrowhead and with water celery; see page 149 for comparison.

New England has about ten species, not easily distinguished, belonging to this genus of native perennials.

Marsh Mermaid Weed
Proserpinaca palustris
Water milfoil family
Height: 6"- 20"
During the cold months, stems from the preceding growing season send out underwater shoots with foliage resembling that of water milfoil. In the spring, marsh mermaid weed emerges from the water and sprouts toothed leaves. By summer the whole plant may be out of the water. A three-cornered, nutlike fruit grows at the base of many leaves.

Marsh Mermaid Weed

Royal Fern

Royal Fern
Osmunda regalis
Flowering fern family
Height: 2'- 4'
The leaflets of the royal fern are widely spaced oblongs lacking the lacy appearance of the "finer" ferns. The leaves are pale green where they grow in sunlight and bright green with reddish stalks in shadier locations. Fertile leaves bear light-brown, flowerlike, spore-bearing leaflets at their tips. Royal fern grows in wet habitats on every continent except Antarctica.

Cinnamon Fern
Osmunda cinnamomea
Glowering fern family
Height: 1'- 4'
Cinnamon fern is the most numerous fern in wet locations, especially along streambanks and in swamps. In late spring, special cinnamon-colored leaves appear; these are the spore-bearing leaves. Fiddleheads, as the newly emerging rolled-up fern leaves are called, are covered with silvery hairs which turn brown as leaves expand.

Marsh Fern
Thelypteris palustris (Dryopteris thelypteris)
Fern family
Height: 1'- 2'
Marsh fern is another of the common native ferns. It likes sunny, moist meadows, but is also found in partial shade. Marsh fern is smaller and more delicate than cinnamon fern and it is much lacier than royal fern. Its stem is usually dark at the base. Marsh fern seldom grows in standing water; royal fern frequently does.

Aquatic Plants

Water Lilies and Other Floating Plants

Plants in this family have tuberous stems buried in the mud. Their leaves dampen wave action, reducing disturbances to small life forms in the shallows. Lily pads are a summer home to many animals. Fish seek their shade and shelter, and join with frogs in harvesting some of the lily-pad-loving insects, such as the caterpillars that live in cases cut from water lily leaves. A variety of water beetles also live in the unique environment provided by water lilies.

Yellow Pond Lily (bullhead lily)
Nuphar variegatum
Water lily family
Leaf diameter: 3"- 15"
The blossoms of the yellow pond lily are two inches in diameter, colored as you would expect from its name. Yellow pond lily flowers from June to September .

Indians gathered the rootstocks of yellow pond lily, which can be used like potatoes. Ducks and geese eat this plant's seeds and deer eat its leaves, stems, and flowers. Muskrats eat all of it.

White Water Lily
Nymphaea odorata
Water lily family
Leaf diameter: 4"- 12"
White water lilies have fragrant white or pink flowers that open in the morning and close during the afternoon. The blossoms are three to five inches in diameter; they open from June to September. The leaves are purple on their undersides. The fruit matures under water during the winter.

Ducks eat the seeds of white water lilies. Muskrats eat the rootstocks.

Watershield (purple wen-dock)
Brasenia schreberi
Water lily family
Leaf diameter: 2"- 4"
Watershield is often found with white water lilies. Its small purple flowers appear from June to August. The stems and the undersides of the leaves are coated with a slimy material. The upper surface of watershield leaves is often patterned by the tunnels of small insects called leaf miners.

Ducks eat watershield seeds. Muskrats and beavers eat the starchy rootstock, as did the Indians.

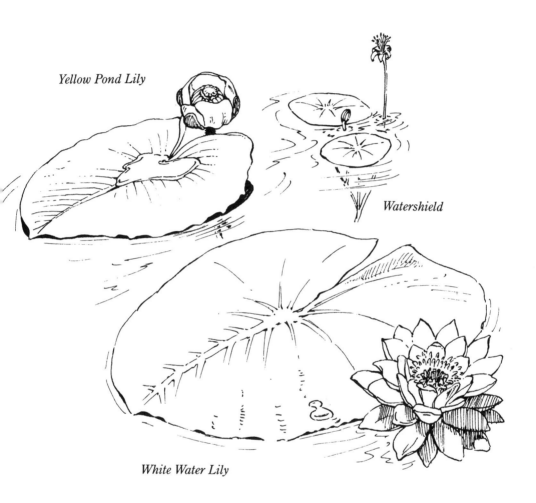

Yellow Pond Lily

Watershield

White Water Lily

Duckweed
Lemna minor and *Spirodela polyrhiza*
Duckweed family
Size: ⅛"- ¼"
In midsummer congregations of these tiny plants form a green blanket on slow-moving water where it is sheltered from the wind. Each leaf of *Lemna* has a single trailing root, whereas *Spirodela* has six or more. Though it occasionally flowers, duckweed usually reproduces by fission. In the fall, mats of green scales break away from the fronds to overwinter on the bottom. Small insects and microscopic organisms dwell in the environment created by duckweed's tiny leaves and roots. When ducks eat duckweed, they ingest these invertebrates along with the plants.

Water-meal
Wolffia columbiana
Duckweed family
Size: 1/32"
Water-meal is the smallest of the flowering plants. The minute flowers form in a pouch on the upper surface of the fronds. Water-meal may become very abundant during June and July, then disappear until the following season.

Water Clover (water shamrock, pepperwort)
Marsilea quadrifolia
Aquatic fern family
Leaf diameter: ½"
Water clover lives in shallow, quiet water, rooted in the mud. It sends up long stems to permit its leaves to float on or near the surface. At night opposite pairs of leaflets fold face to face. Botanically a fern, in appearance water clover is far from what we consider fern-like. Ducks eat the fruiting bodies of water clover, which are brownish, bean-shaped spore capsules.

Water clover was introduced from Europe in 1862 to a lake in Connecticut. It is said to have been introduced to the Concord and Sudbury Rivers from the Harvard Botanical Garden.

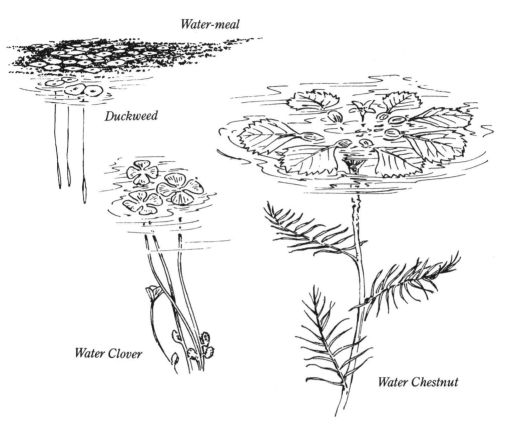

Water-meal

Duckweed

Water Clover

Water Chestnut

Water Chestnut
Trapa natans
Water chestnut family
Leaf diameter: 2"- 3½"
The upper surfaces of floating water chestnut leaves are glossy; their undersides hairy. The small white flowers that appear among the leaves produce spiny nuts that drop to the bottom for the winter. A native of Eurasia, water chestnut became a pest in our rivers during the 1930s. Today it forms broad mats along the Sudbury below Route 20. Water chestnut offers little food for wildlife.

Feathery Submerged Plants

Coontail
Ceratophyllum demersum
Hornwort family
Size: Leaf whorl — 1½" in diameter
Long strands of coontail may be anchored to the bottom, but are without roots. Flowers and seeds grow at the bases of some of the leaves; they are usually hard to find. This common plant aids fish by supporting insects and sheltering fry. In late summer the ends of the branches break off and fall to the bottom; in the spring these rise to the surface to begin the new season's growth. Waterfowl, caterpillars, and other invertebrates feed on coontail.

Fanwort
Cabomba caroliniana
Water lily family
Size: fan-shaped leaves 1½" wide
The lacy submerged leaves of *Cabomba* lend a warm green to the water in many places along the lower Sudbury and the Concord Rivers. Small white flowers emerge in late summer, amid tiny floating leaves. Fanwort is native to the United States but not to Massachusetts; it is naturalized from farther south. It provides cover and food for fish.

Low Watermilfoil
Myriophyllum humile
Watermilfoil family
Size: Leaves — 1" long
Watermilfoil leaves take different forms according to whether they are submerged or exposed to the atmosphere. Water hemlock, a stouter member of the same family, behaves similarly. Tiny flowers are at the base of some leaves of watermilfoil. When the plant disintegrates in the fall, a small roll of unexpanded shoots drops to the bottom and overwinters. Many insects feed on this rooted aquatic plant.

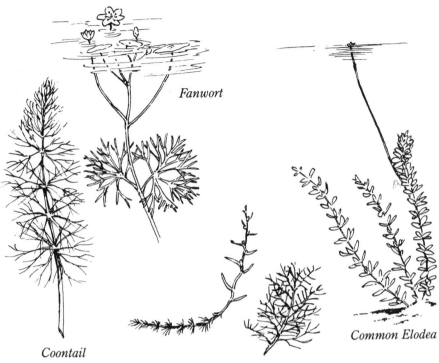

Fanwort

Common Elodea

Coontail

Low Watermilfoil

Common Elodea (waterweed, frogbit)
Elodea nuttallii
Frog bit family
Size: leaves approximately ½″ long
The leaves of elodea are broader and flatter than those of the other feathery aquatic plants. Elodea is normally rooted, but may break off to form floating mats. The stems are sometimes tinged with purple. Tiny white or pink flowers float on the surface, connected to stems by long stalks. Elodea provides shelter and support for aquatic insects. It is eaten by ducks, beavers, and muskrats. A prodigious producer of oxygen, elodea is used by science teachers to demonstrate the production of this gas during photosynthesis.

147

Ribbon-leaved Plants

Water Celery (wild celery, eelgrass)
Vallisneria americana
Frogbit family
Size: leaves ½" wide, 3' long.
Clusters of the ribbonlike leaves of water celery grow from a creeping rootstock. The upper part of the leaves may be floating. Male flowers grow in a cluster at the base of the leaves. When mature they break loose and float to the surface where floating female flowers are waiting, tethered to long stems. After pollination, the stem contracts, pulling the fruit down into the water, where the seeds mature. The stems and fruits provide food for waterfowl. The leaves support insects and shelter fish.

Variable Pondweed
Potamogeton natans and other species
Pondweed family
Pondweeds are common in our rivers. Their leaves vary in width and shape, even on the same plant. Floating leaves are broader and blunter than submerged leaves —but rising water submerges both. Flowering catkins emerge in late summer. In New England, the genus *Potamogeton* has about thirty species whose leaves vary in form from circular to hairlike. Plants in our rivers that have alternately placed leaves and jointed stems are likely to be pondweed.

Caterpillars make cases of pondweed, fly larvae mine its leaves, and birds, muskrats, beaver, and deer feed upon it.

Burreed
This emergent plant often finds itself under water along the rivers. See page 139 for description.

Arrowhead
Ribbonlike leaves precede arrowhead leaves, the latter emerging after the water level drops. Arrowhead leaves assume a variety of shapes within the same species; the grass-leaved form is pictured here. See page 133 for description.

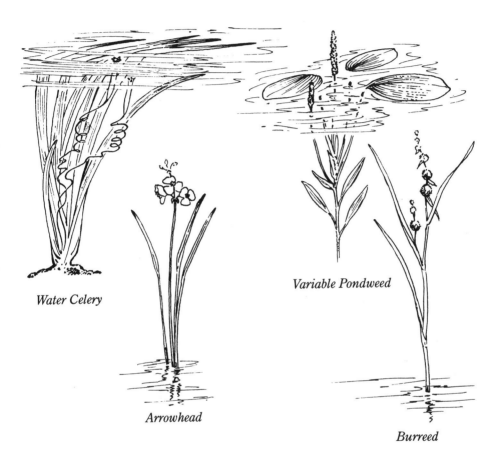

Water Celery

Arrowhead

Variable Pondweed

Burreed

Animals

Early in their lives children develop an interest in animals that mixes intense sympathy toward some species with irrational fears about others. In a few people, this combination of attitudes persists throughout adulthood. It may be replaced by open-minded appreciation... or by a callous disregard. In the past, as occasionally in the present, humans destroyed the lives of animals without any sense of what was being lost, as if it were a good bargain to trade the life of a heron for a few of his feathers. There is evidence that we are now prepared to weigh such transactions with greater care, and with some love for the creatures obliged to share their Earth with us.

Birds

Birds Seen Along Wooded Riverbanks

Belted Kingfisher
Megaceryle alcyon
Kingfisher family
Length: 11"-15"
The belted kingfisher is the only kingfisher of northeastern America. Both sexes are blue-gray above and white below, with a blue-gray breast band. Females have a chestnut belly band as well.

Kingfishers often announce their approach with their loud, rattling call: *rickety, crick, crick, crick.* Sometimes the first sign of their presence is a loud splash, followed seconds later by the emergence of a kingfisher from the water.

Typically they hunt perched on a dead branch over the water, but kingfishers can hover over the surface like terns. The staple of their diet is small fish. They also eat crayfish, frogs, small snakes, turtles, mussels, insects, young birds, and mice. Pellets of fishbones, scales, and other indigestible parts of food are disgorged.

The nest is in a burrow dug into a sheer soil bank, which may be a riverbank but can also be a road cut or gravel pit far from water. The burrow is four inches in diameter and three to seven feet long.

In the warm months, kingfishers are usually easy to find on the lower Assabet, and locally throughout the basin. They winter in Massachusetts and southward, seeking open water and adequate prey.

Belted Kingfisher

Common Flicker
Colaptes auratus
Woodpecker family
Length: 12″-14″

The common flicker's back and wings are brown, barred with black; a black crescent crosses its upper breast. The white front is covered with black spots. The head is tawny. The male has a gray and red crown. When it flies up from the ground, where it usually feeds, its white rump patch is conspicuous. Nothing looks like a flicker except a flicker. Its call is a loud, emphatic *wicka, wicka, wicka.*

Flickers eat mainly ants, other insects, and some berries and seeds. In the spring, the male digs a nest cavity in the trunk of a dead tree. The female lays five to ten white eggs on fresh chips at the bottom of the hole. Flickers are common summer residents in Massachusetts and migrants in spring and fall. They winter in southern North America.

Eastern Kingbird
Tyrannus tyrannus
Flycatcher family
Length: 8″
Kingbirds, so named for their fearless attacks on hawks, crows, and even low-flying airplanes, are common summer residents. The head, back, and tail are black. A broad band of white at the tip of the tail is the best mark for field identification. The underside is white, with a pale gray band across the breast.

Kingbirds make a rapid sputter of high-pitched notes: *tzi, tzee, tzi, tzee, tzi, tzee.* They catch insects in the typical flycatcher fashion, flying out from a perch to snap them from the air. Sometimes kingbirds scoop insects from the surface of the water. Kingbirds pick berries by hovering. They nest on a tree limb, in low shrubs along the water's edge, or on stumps or snags above water. Eastern kingbirds head to South America beginning in August and return in early May.

Downy Woodpecker
Picoides pubescens
Woodpecker family
Length: 6″
Downy woodpeckers may be distinguished from the similar hairy woodpecker by their smaller size and much smaller bill. They are black and white. Males have a red spot on the back of the head. Downies eat insects, berries, acorns, and nuts. Their call note is an unemphatic *pick*. They are common residents throughout the year.

Yellow Warbler
Dendroica petechia
Wood warbler family
Length: 5″
Sweet, sweet, sweeterer-than-sweet bursts the yellow warbler in May and June.

Bright yellow in front, appearing *all* yellow from a distance, this tiny bird makes itself visible and difficult to ignore through its persistent, optimistic song. With the aid of binoculars, one sees that the back is dulled with olive, and the breast streaked with chestnut. Yellow warblers eat caterpillars, including gypsy moth caterpillars, and many other insects. Their nest is in the forking branches of a bush or sapling. They winter from Mexico to northern South America.

Yellow warblers are often victimized by brown-headed cowbirds. Female cowbirds lay their eggs in the nests of "hosts." The warbler parents raise the cowbird chicks at the expense of their own.

White-breasted Nuthatch
Sitta carolinensis
Nuthatch family
Length: 6″
White-breasted nuthatches are pearl gray above. Their faces and undersides are white. Both sexes have black collar-like bands across their shoulders. On males this extends forward to form a black crown; females have grayer crowns. The crispness of their movements lends nuthatches an executive quality; they seem confident and self-possessed. They are usually seen patrolling tree trunks from top to bottom, head first. In the winter they search the bark of trees and the eaves and shingles of houses for dormant insects. White-breasted nuthatches are common permanent residents.

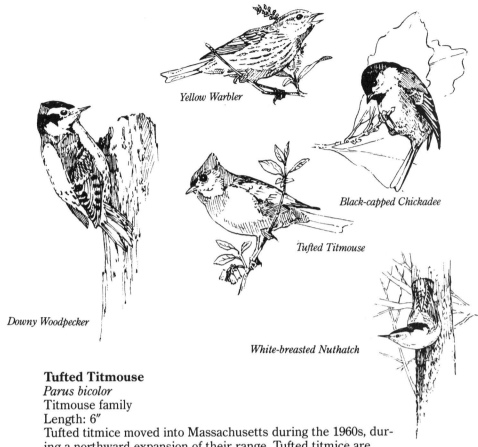

Yellow Warbler

Black-capped Chickadee

Tufted Titmouse

Downy Woodpecker

White-breasted Nuthatch

Tufted Titmouse
Parus bicolor
Titmouse family
Length: 6″
Tufted titmice moved into Massachusetts during the 1960s, during a northward expansion of their range. Tufted titmice are gray above and white below. They whistle *peter, peter, peter.*

Titmice eat insects and seeds. To line their nests, which are in tree cavities, they take hairs from live woodchucks, squirrels, opossums, and, sometimes, people. They remain in Massachusetts year-round, and they frequent bird-feeders.

Black-capped chickadee
Parus atricapillus
Titmouse family
Length: 5″
A common permanent resident, the black-capped chickadee is our state bird. Their *chick-a-dee-dee-dee* is familiar to anyone who pays any attention to birds. They frequent winter feeding stations. Chickadees are gregarious, travelling through the fall and winter woods in bands with tufted titmice, nuthatches, and downy woodpeckers. Chickadees nest in tree cavities they excavate themselves, or use woodpecker holes or nest boxes. They have been known to live twelve years, but average only two to three. They weigh a third of an ounce.

155

Wood Thrush
Hylocichla mustelina
Thrush family
Length: 8"
The canoeist is much more likely to hear a wood thrush singing than to see one. The song of the wood thrush is a sweet, flutelike, unhurried *ee-oh-lee, ee-oh-lay*. The species is slightly smaller than its close relative, the robin. Wood thrushes forage for insects and other invertebrates on the forest floor and nest on or near the ground.

Gray Catbird
Dumetella carolinensis
Mimic thrush family
Length: 9"
Catbirds are gray with black caps. They mimic the songs of other birds, and intersperse a unique mewing that suggests their name. Catbirds are curious about humans. Their interest in us makes them seem clever. Perhaps they *are* smarter than other songbirds: they usually recognize cowbird eggs and push them from their nests. Catbirds are common summer residents. They return from the tropics in early May.

Cedar Waxwing
Bombycilla cedrorum
Waxwing family
Length: 7"
Cedar waxwings are tan. Their shading makes them appear to glow. They have a bright yellow band at the tip of their tails. Their crisp lines and vivid details make them dapper. They are named for the waxy red tips on a row of their wing feathers, the function of which is not known. Waxwings are usually seen in groups, their high-pitched thin *zeeees* overlapping and continuous.

Northern (Baltimore) Oriole
Icterus galbula galbula
Blackbird family
Length: 8"
Male Baltimore orioles are bright orange and black. Females and young are olive above, and warm yellow below. Canoeists may spot male orioles singing a loud, cheerful, whistled song from conspicuous perches above the rivers in late May and June. Orioles build woven bag nests that hang from the tips of tree branches high over the ground. They winter in the American tropics.

Wood Thrush

Common Yellowthroat

Gray Catbird

Northern (Baltimore) Oriole

Cedar Waxwing

Common Yellowthroat
Geothylpis trichas
Wood warbler family
Length: 5″

The common yellowthroat is abundant here as it is across the continent. Both sexes have a bright yellow throat and olive-green back. Males have a vivid black facial mask that makes identification easy. Common in thickets near our rivers, their *witchity-witchity-witchy-witch* signals the presence of a yellowthroat. Like many songbirds, the yellowthroat will often show itself in response to a hissing *psss pzzz pssss* call from a human.

Tree Swallow

Iridoprocne bicolor
Swallow family
Length: 5"- 6"

Tree swallows are metallic blue-black
or green-black above and snow white
below. The voice is a liquid twitter.
They spend their summers catching
insects over open water, marshes, or
meadows. They nest in tree cavities
or birdhouses. They fret over their
nests, working on them for weeks,
then lining them with feathers that
they collect or steal from each other.

Tree swallows will feed on berries,
which allows them to winter farther
north than other swallows. They nest
in large numbers in the dead trees in
the Assabet Reservoir.

Common Grackle
Quiscalus quiscula
Blackbird family
Length: 11″- 13½″
Common grackles are large iridescent blackbirds with yellow eyes and long wedge-shaped tails. They are present, visibly and audibly, along the river banks throughout the spring, summer, and fall. Their call is a loud *chack,* their song rasping and harsh. They eat seeds, worms, insects, and small vertebrates, including snakes, birds, fish, and bats.

Birds Seen Near Fields or Pastures

Bobolink
Dolichonyx oryzivorus
Blackbird family
Length: 6"- 8"
In their breeding plumage, male bobolinks have black heads, wings, and undersides, white backs, and yellow napes. In the winter males resemble females, which are tawny below, brownish above, and have brown bands over their eyes. The bobolink song is exuberant, bubbly, and variable.

Bobolinks nest on the ground in grasslands. They nest on Orchard Hill (AS mile 16.3) in Stow, where they are not thwarted by early mowing of the hay. They may be seen moving through the river meadows during fall migration. Bobolinks make a long migration — they winter in southern South America.

American Woodcock
Philohela minor
Sandpiper family
Length: 11"
Woodcocks are buffy below and marked above in gray, tan, and brown.

In springtime woodcocks make marvelous flight displays at dusk and dawn, over fields or pastures. From the ground they make a loud *peent* call, at intervals, as if gathering a crowd for the performance to follow. They fly 300 feet into the faintly lit sky, then descend in zigzags, accompanying themselves with a "song" produced by air passing over their wing feathers. Back on the ground, they resume their *peent*. When the moon is bright, this sequence may be repeated for many hours.

Song Sparrow
Melospiza melodia
Finch family
Length: 5"- 6"
Song sparrows are brown above, white with streaks below. They have a dark central spot on their breasts. These abundant birds inhabit thickets at edges of meadows, marshes, roads, or lawns. They are aptly named, because they are talented singers. Most song sparrows migrate to southern states for the winter, but some stay with us throughout the year.

Bobolink

Song Sparrow

American Woodcock

Barn Swallow

Killdeer

Killdeer
Charadrius vociferus
Plover family
Length: 9″-11″
The killdeer is named for one of its calls, a high-pitched *kill-deeeah*. This is the common inland plover. The white breast is double-banded in black. In flight, the wings bear a striking pattern of brown, white, and black, and the tawny rump is visible.

The nest is on the ground, in the open, protected by the superb camouflage of the eggs and by the crippled-bird act the adults use to lure away predators.

Barn Swallow
Hirundo rustica
Swallow family
Length: 6″- 8″
The throat of the barn swallow is chestnut, the undersides buff, and the back iridescent blue-black. There are white spots on the dark, forked tail.

Barn swallows feed over fields such as Orchard Hill (AS mile 16.3), where they live in the big, century-old barn facing Gleasondale. They also feed over open water, as at the pool below Tyler Dam. They are abundant migrants through the river meadows, and are common summer residents.

Birds Seen Near Marshes

Red-winged Blackbird
Agelaius phoeniceus
Blackbird family
Length: 7"- 9"
Red-winged blackbirds are named after the appearance of the males. Females are broadly striped with grayish-brown, tan, and black.

The cry of the red-wing, heard at every marsh throughout the spring and early summer, is usually given as *O-ka-LEEEE!*, but is more easily remembered as *prop-er-TEEEE!* when associated with the territoriality of the males. Males occupy territories before the females return from winter quarters. More than one female may nest within the domain of a male; they are polygamous.

Red-wings are common along the rivers from early spring through July. They become hard to find in August, but reappear in September.

Marsh Wren
Cistothorus palustris
Wren family
Length: 5″

Marsh wrens are white underneath. Their upper sides are shades of brown. They have white eye stripes and black and white stripes on their upper backs. Their lively songs include trills, rattles, and reedy notes. They live in cattail or bulrush marshes, feeding on insects. Each male has several mates in his territory. Males build a series of dummy nests. Females build the nests in which they actually lay eggs. The nests are globular structures of reeds and grasses with an entrance at the side. Marsh wrens winter in the southern United States and Mexico.

The marsh wren population has declined in our river marshes in the past thirty years, for unknown reasons. They nest in the marsh drained by Wash Brook (SU mile 20).

American Bittern
Botaurus lentiginosus
Heron family
Length: 23″

American bitterns are stocky brown birds. As they stand among marsh plants with their bills pointed skyward, their brown breast stripes blend with the sedge and cattails they inhabit. The loud deep song is a pumping *pump-ER-lunk*. Bitterns feed on fish and other small animals. They nest individually, not in colonies. The area between the Sudbury River and Heard Pond (SU mile 18.1) is a good place to look and listen for bitterns.

Great Blue Heron
Ardea herodias
Heron family
Length: 42"-52"
Great blue herons have tan and white necks, blue-gray backs and wings, yellow bills, and dull olive legs. Their voice is a loud harsh squawk: *frawnk, frawnk, frawnk.*

They nest in colonies, usually in tall trees. One colony is in the Assabet Reservoir in Westborough. It should be viewed from a distance, to avoid startling the birds.

Great blue herons eat any small animals they can catch and swallow, which makes a long list including fish, frogs, crayfish, insects, and mice. They hunt by wading along the edge of bodies of water such as our rivers.

Great blue herons have profited by protection from shooting. We see them more often than did William Brewster at the turn of the century.

Green-backed Heron
Butorides striatus
Heron family
Length: 16"- 22"
The green-backed heron's neck is chestnut, and its back and wings gray-green or gray-blue. Its voice is a loud *skeow.*

Green-backed herons nest in swamps or woods, usually singly but sometimes in small colonies. Their diet consists of small fish, insects, tadpoles, worms, and snails. They seem curious about humans. When put to flight they often land while still in view, as if to observe the human intruder.

Green-backed herons winter between the southern United States and northern South America.

Black-crowned Night Heron

Green-backed Heron

Great Blue Heron

Black-crowned Night Heron
Nycticorax nycticorax
Heron family
Length: 23"- 28"
The back of the head and body is black, the front is white, and the wings gray. Juveniles are streaked brown. The voice of the black-crowned night heron is a loud *squawk*, often heard at dusk along the Concord and lower Sudbury.

Black-crowned night herons nest in colonies in a variety of habitats, usually on an island. Like the other herons, black-crowns live on a diet of small animals, primarily fish. Night herons are so called because, unlike other herons, they do most of their hunting at night. Black-crowned night herons are more frequently seen in the lower part of the basin than the upper.

Ducks

Wood Duck
Aix sponsa
Duck family
Length: 17"- 20"
In their breeding plumage, male wood ducks are colorfully marked. The eyes and bill are red, the head is iridescent green, and the chest brown. The female's head is gray, with a large white eye-ring. The female's call is a loud, oft-repeated *weeek, weeek, weeek.*

Wood ducks frequently perch in trees. They nest in hollow trees, large woodpecker holes, or nest boxes. The day they hatch, the ducklings plummet to the ground or into the water. Wood ducks eat aquatic plants, acorns, and insects.

The Concord Basin offers fine wood duck habitat and supports a large population.

Black Duck
Anas rubripes
Duck family
Length: 21"- 25"
Males and females are similar. They are dark brown, with heads slightly lighter. The silver wing lining is a distinctive field mark. Females quack like mallards.

Nests are in marsh grass, under bushes, or in wooded swamps. Black ducks have a varied diet including aquatic plants, worms, mollusks, and acorns.

Mallard
Anas platyrhynchos
Duck family
Length: 20"- 28"
Mallard males have iridescent green heads and chestnut breasts. Females are mottled brown. Female mallards quack loudly.

Nests are on the ground, usually near water. Mallards eat aquatic plants supplemented with some aquatic animals.

Mallards are common throughout the Concord Basin, as they are in temperate climates throughout the northern hemisphere. They are the ancestors of most breeds of domestic ducks.

Wood Duck

Black Duck

Mallard

Blue-winged Teal

Blue-winged Teal
Anas discors
Duck family
Length: 15″
Blue-winged teal are mottled gray-brown, with chalky blue patches on their wings. Males may peep softly when flying. Females quack weakly. Their nests are in tall grass on dry ground near water, or in dense cattails. The diet is seventy percent plant food, such as the seeds of sedges and smartweeds, and thirty percent snails, insects, and crustaceans. Blue-winged teal are often abundant at Great Meadows in the fall.

167

Ring-necked Duck
Aythya collaris
Duck family
Length: 15"- 18"
Male ring-necks have purple iridescence on a blackish head. Their backs and breasts are black; the sides are gray. The chestnut neck ring is not normally visible. The female is brown. Ring-necked ducks are usually silent. Their diet includes the seeds of aquatic plants, snails, and insects.

Ring-necks may be abundant on the rivers in the spring; look for them as soon as the ice goes out.

Common Merganser
Mergus merganser
Duck family
Length: 22"- 27"
The male's head is green, the bill and feet are red, the back is black, and the sides and breast white. The female's head is brown, her body gray. The voice is a low rasping croak. Mergansers dive for fish, which they grasp with the sawlike edges of their bills.

Common mergansers often pause at Great Meadows and along the rivers during their spring migration flight to nesting grounds farther north. They also appear in late fall before freeze-up and on openings all winter.

Pied-billed Grebe
Podilymbus podiceps
Grebe family
Length: 13"
Pied-billed grebes are brown. In spring and summer the bill is whitish, with a black band. The voice is a series of hollow notes: *kud-kuk-kuk-cow-cow-coup-coup.* They eat fish, crustaceans, and insects. They escape from danger by sinking slowly out of sight into the water, then taking cover in vegetation.

168

Pied-billed Grebe

Ring-necked Duck

Common Merganser

Birds of Prey

Osprey
Pandion haliaetus
Osprey family
Length: 21"- 24"
The osprey is brown and white. Its cry is a series of high-pitched whistles: *cheap, cheap, cheap*.

Nests are bulky constructions in trees or on platforms set up on high poles. The Sudbury Valley Trustees erected a nest platform near the Lincoln canoe launch that has not yet been occupied. Ospreys eat fish, which they catch on the wing, plunging feet first into the water, seizing prey in their talons. Ospreys are not numerous along our rivers, but appear regularly as migrants along the Concord, the lower Sudbury, and the Assabet in Stow and Hudson.

Red-tailed Hawk
Buteo jamaicensis
Hawk family
Length: 19″- 25″′
This large hawk is dark brown above, white below, with brown streaks. The tail is bright rufous above, paler below. The red-tail's cry is a pene- trating, confident *ker,* slurred downward.

The nest is in a tree, usually high above the ground. Red-tails eat rodents, plus some grasshoppers, birds, and snakes. Red-tails are the hawks most likely to be seen in the Concord Basin. They are year-round residents throughout, usually seen perched on a dead stub or soaring high overhead.

Broad-winged Hawk
Buteo platypterus
Hawk family
Length: 14″— 19″
The broad-wing's tail is banded black and white. The underside of the breast is white with light streaking; the back is brown. The broad-wing's cry is a shrill *pweeee.*

Broad-wings usually nest in woods, high in a tree. They prey on toads, frogs, snakes, squirrels, chipmunks, insects, and other small animals. They are most often seen in the Concord Basin during fall migration, in flocks of five to fifteen birds. At concen- tration points such as Mount Wachusett they appear in much larger numbers on peak days in September.

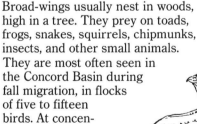

171

American Kestrel
Falco sparverius
Falcon family
Length: 9"-12"
Kestrels have mottled brown backs and their breasts are white or buff with dark streaks. Males have blue-gray wings. The tails of both sexes are reddish-brown. The call is *killy, killy, killy.*

Kestrels nest in tree cavities such as holes previously used by flickers. They eat birds, insects, and other small animals. Kestrels hover on fast-beating wings while hunting.

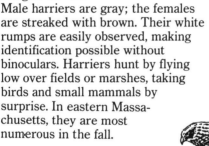

Northern Harrier (marsh hawk)
Circus cyaneus
Hawk family
Length: 18"- 24"
Male harriers are gray; the females are streaked with brown. Their white rumps are easily observed, making identification possible without binoculars. Harriers hunt by flying low over fields or marshes, taking birds and small mammals by surprise. In eastern Massachusetts, they are most numerous in the fall.

Fish

Brook Trout
Salvelinus fontinalis
Trout family
Length: to 21″; typically 6″- 14″
Brook trout have unbordered yellow spots interspersed with
red spots inside blue aureoles. They are native to the northeastern United States. They eat primarily aquatic insects. Brookies
spawn in cool streams in the fall. A few natural populations
maintain themselves in brooks in the Concord Basin.

Brook trout are caught on flies, small spinners, worms, and
bright foods. They are rather gullible. The Massachusetts Division of Fisheries and Wildlife stocks brook trout in the upper
Sudbury and in tributaries of the Assabet. Rainbow and brown
trout are also stocked in these waters.

Largemouth Bass
Micropterus salmoides
Sunfish family
Length: to 25″; typically 6″- 20″
Largemouths are dark green above, shading to gold below the
dark stripe on their sides. They thrive in shallow, weedy lakes
like the Assabet Reservoir, and river backwaters such as the
vanes of stillwater that project from the Assabet above Hudson.
The lower Sudbury and the Concord offer fine bass habitat.
Some trophy fish (eight pounds and up) are taken from Heard
Pond and the Concord River each year.

Largemouths spawn in the late spring. Males build nests in
places where the water is two feet deep. The nest is a shallow
depression in the bottom. Males aerate the eggs by fanning the
water with their tails.

Bass are aggressive predators. They eat crayfish, fish, frogs,
and other small animals.

Bass are good to eat, but even better to catch, so sportspeople
often release them to fight another day. In the lower Sudbury
the fish are contaminated and must not be eaten. (See page
115.)

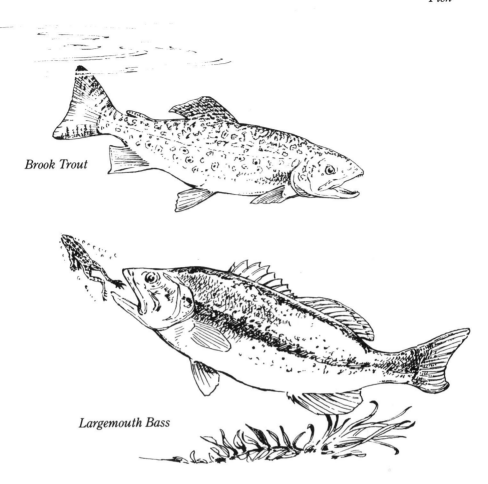

Brook Trout

Largemouth Bass

Brown Bullhead (hornpout, catfish)
Ictalurus nebulosus
Catfish family
Length: to 19″; typically 6″- 12″
The back is olive or brown, and the sides lighter but mottled with brown. Brown bullheads feed mostly at night, tasting their way along the dark river bottoms with receptors on their barbels. Fairhaven Bay provides good bullhead habitat. Omnivores, bullheads eat more plant material than most fishes, but also take small fish, insect larvae, and crustaceans.

Brown Bullhead

175

Chain Pickerel
Esox niger
Pike family
Length: to 31"; typically 7"- 20"
As you fish the lily pads of the Sudbury behind Saxonville Dam, or the weedy sloughs of the Assabet, these long-bodied, sharp-toothed predators may strike from their weedy lairs. Pickerel have olive markings on a gold field; their similar cousins, northern pike, have golden, bean-shaped spots on an olive background.

Black Crappie (calico bass)
Pomoxis nigromaculatus
Sunfish family
Length: to 16"; typically 5"- 12"
These scrappy black and silver fish are found in all three of our rivers. Some call them calico bass, thus avoiding the question of whether to pronounce crappie as "croppie" or "crappie." Crappie prefer still or sluggish waters such as the impoundments above dams.

Yellow Perch
Perca flavescens
Perch family
Length: to 15"; typically 6"- 11"
Yellow perch are yellow with black bands. The lower fins are sometimes bright red. Yellow perch travel in schools. They are found in deep water, as at Fairhaven Bay. They are sought with live bait, but it is not unusual to catch one on a spinner or other lure.

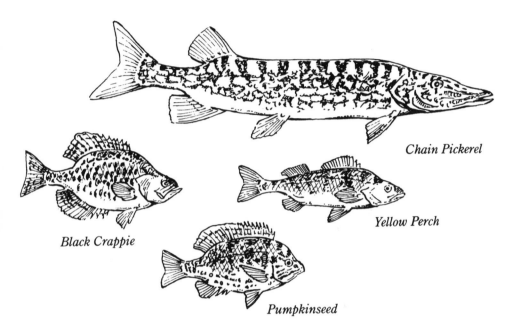

Chain Pickerel

Black Crappie

Yellow Perch

Pumpkinseed

Pumpkinseed
Lepomis gibbosus
Sunfish family
Length: to 10″
The pumpkinseed is olive above and red, blue, green, and yellow below. The black gill cover has a bright red spot at the tip. The similar bluegill is less vividly colored and lacks the red spot on the gill cover. Both species live in quiet, weedy waters. They build saucer-shaped nests in sand and gravel in shallow water. Nests are guarded by the males. Pumpkinseeds eat insects and small fish.

OTHER FISH not pictured but present in Concord Basin rivers include northern pike, American eel, white sucker, carp, golden shiner, white perch, and many smaller species.

Mammals

Red Fox
Vulpes vulpes
Dog family
Weight: 8 - 15 lbs.

Red foxes are rusty above and white underneath, with dark legs and feet. Their tails are tipped with white. Color variations occur, but all red foxes have the white-tipped tail. The gray fox, a different species that also inhabits the Concord Basin, lacks the white tip.

Red foxes seek a territory with a variety of habitats including field, orchard, and woods. The diversity of the eastern Massachusetts landscape is well suited to foxes. Their diet is primarily small mammals, birds, fruits, and insects. Fox hunting routes often parallel stone walls, which shelter multitudes of small mammals: mice, voles, chipmunks, and shrews.

Kits are born in the spring, in a den in a bank, hillside, or rock pile. Active throughout the year, foxes are solitary until the midwinter breeding season. The families disperse in August. Foxes are cautious and learn from experience. Their needs for food and water bring them to riversides, where they are most likely to be seen in the twilight of morning or evening, or sunning at midday. Fox populations fluctuate, as do those of all animals. Even when they are numerous, foxes are skillful at avoiding contact with humans.

Muskrat
Ondatra zibethicus
Rodent family
Weight: 1- 4 lbs
The muskrat's fur is dark brown, and its tail in seven to twelve inches long, sparsely haired, scaly, and vertically flattened. Muskrats eat vegetation such as cattails, rushes, sedges, water lilies, and pond weeds. They occasionally eat crayfish, frogs, clams, and fish. Females in our region give birth to about three litters a year, with an average of five young per litter.

Complex systems of tunnels in riverbanks serve muskrats as den sites and travel routes. If high banks are not available for burrowed dens, muskrats build houses similar to beaver lodges, made of cattails and other aquatic plants. Because they prefer swimming to walking, they build canals that enable them to swim through marshes.

Muskrats can stay underwater for longer than ten minutes. They are preyed upon by mink and raccoons, and, of course, by humans, who trap them in large numbers for their fur.

Though primarily nocturnal, muskrats are often active in daytime. They are the wild mammal most likely to be seen by the canoeist.

179

Raccoon

Procyon lotor
Panda family
Weight: 12-48 lbs

Raccoons are grayish brown. Their name comes from the Algonquin *aroughcoune,* meaning "he scratches with his hands." The omnivorous raccoon eats all kinds of small animals, bird and turtle eggs, and a wide variety of vegetable food. Raccoons forage at night along streams and river-banks, leaving tracks that look like those of miniature human hands. Litters of about five young are born in May and leave the den two months later.

The heavy toll of young raccoons taken on our roads is an indication of the thorough-ness with which these adaptable animals have accommodated to survival within sub-urban areas. Human refuse augments or replaces other food sources, and larger pre-dators have been driven to wilder locales. Automobiles claim some of the resulting surplus population of raccoons.

Mink
Mustela vison
Weasel family
Weight: 1½- 3½ lbs

These dark-furred weasels are numerous in the Concord Basin. They often prey on aquatic animals, so they are usually found near water. They eat muskrats, chipmunks, rabbits, young snapping turtles, marsh birds, and fish. They den near water, in old muskrat burrows or hollow logs. Fierce predators, they are themselves the prey of great horned owls, foxes, and bobcats.

Mink are active in winter. When on land they are easy to spot as they scamper across ice and snow. The young are born in the spring and disperse in the fall.

River Otter
Lutra canadensis
Weasel family
Weight: 11-30 lbs

River otters are dark brown. They eat mostly fish. They are most active from dawn to mid-morning, and in the evening. Their curiosity, playfulness, sociability, and the coy expression lent by their big eyes and whiskers make otters seem rather human. Litters of one to four blind and helpless young are born early in the spring.

Otters are thought to be increasing in number. They are occasionally seen in the Concord Basin, but are not well-established residents like mink and muskrats.

White-tailed Deer
Odocoileus virginianus
Deer family
Weight: 150 - 300 lbs
White-tails are our only deer. They are tan in summer and
grayish in winter. Their bellies and throats are white. The
fawns are spotted. Males grow new antlers each year, which are
shed in late winter and quickly consumed by rodents for the
minerals they contain.

Signs of white-tail habitation include the ragged nibbled ends of
greenbriar and other plants, the pelletlike scat, and "buckrubs."
Buckrubs are sections of small trees, two or three feet above
the ground, which have been rubbed clean of bark by antlers.
Buckrubs are produced as part of the territorial behavior that
occurs in the fall breeding season. Deer are active and feeding
all winter. In times of deep snow they "yard up" in sheltered
locations such as groves of hemlock. Does give birth to one or
two fawns late in the spring.

White-tails are able to live in close association with humans, if
there is suitable habitat. They live in the Concord Basin
wherever orchards, fields, and forests remain.

Little Brown Bat
Myotis lucifugus
Plain-nosed bat family
Weight: ⅛ - ½ oz.
At least eight different bat species live in the Concord Basin.
The little brown bat is shown because it is one of the most com-
mon. It is usually seen in the evening, hunting insects by
echolocation.

In summer, little brown bats form nursery colonies in buildings.
In winter they hibernate in caves and mines that may be hun-
dreds of miles from their breeding grounds.

*OTHER MAMMALS not pictured but present in or along the
rivers include the occasional beaver, increasing numbers of eastern
coyotes, and innumerable mice, shrews, rats, and voles that sustain
predators such as hawks and foxes.*

Reptiles and Amphibians

Reptiles

Snapping Turtle
Chelydra serpentina
Snapping and musk turtle family
Length: 8" - 18"
Weight: to 45 lbs.
The snapping turtle's upper shell, the carapace, is tan to dark brown; the lower shell, the plastron, is yellow to tan. Snappers eat worms, crayfish, carrion, aquatic plants, fish, birds, and small mammals. They are not destructive to natural populations of fish or birds. When disturbed in water, snappers disappear into the depths, or, if trapped in the shallows, retract their heads. On land, they snap in self-defense.

It is not unusual to see large snappers in shallow water in the upper Assabet and Sudbury. They live throughout the basin, but are less frequently observed in deep water. Females are often seen on land in May or June, when they emerge to lay eggs. Many of their eggs are devoured by raccoons and other mammals.

Snapping turtles are one of nature's finest survivors. They possess great hardiness. Snappers prosper by using energy sparingly and by eating whatever comes along. . .a philosophy tested by the ages. Snapping turtle bones have been found by archaeologists in excavations of the camps of ancient humans. Snappers are sometimes used as food today, particularly in turtle soup.

Painted Turtle
Chrysemys picta
Pond and box turtle family
Length: 4"- 6"
Painted turtles have yellow spots on the sides of their heads and red markings on the fringes of their carapaces. They are the common basking turtles of our rivers. Young painted turtles eat mostly aquatic invertebrates and carrion. Mature turtles eat fifty percent plant material, plus carrion, insects, mussels, snails, and fish. They are most active in the daytime.

Female painted turtles lay five or six eggs in a sandy bank during May, June, or July. Hatchlings emerge two and half months later. Raccoons, skunks, and mink eat the eggs; baby turtles are preyed upon by herons, kingfishers, and a host of other predators.

Snapping Turtle

Blandings Turtle
Emydoidea blandingii
Pond and box turtle family
Length: 5"- 7"

Blandings turtles have a bright yellow chin and throat. The dome-like carapace has many small tan spots. The plastron is hinged. These rare turtles are listed as "threatened" by the Massachusetts Natural Heritage Program; seeing one is a special treat.

Females lay eight or nine eggs in June or July. These hatch in autumn or the following spring. Blandings turtles depend on crayfish for as much as fifty percent of their diet; the remaining half is other invertebrates and some plants. They leave the water to dine upon insects and snails. Blandings turtles remain active at lower temperatures than most turtles.

The Spotted Turtle, not pictured, also resides in our rivers. It is somewhat smaller than the painted turtle, which it otherwise resembles in form and habits. The carapaces of spotted turtles have many small yellow spots. The Massachusetts Natural Heritage Program regards this species as "of special concern."

Painted Turtle

Blandings Turtle

185

Eastern Garter Snake
Thamnophis sirtalis
Length: to 26″
Garter snakes' stripes are usually yellow but may be tan, green, or bluish. This common snake adapts to many habitats. Garter snakes eat frogs, toads, insects, salamanders, and earthworms. They mate in the spring, and bear one-half dozen to several dozen live young during the summer.

The RIBBON SNAKE, another member of the garter snake genus, is sometimes found swimming across the surface of our rivers. Ribbon snakes like to bask in shrubs overhanging water. In appearance they closely resemble eastern garter snakes.

Northern Water Snake
Nerodia sipedon
Length: to 42″
Adult water snakes become so dark that their markings are hard to see. They may be gray, brown, or black. Water snakes eat small fish and frogs.

The northern water snake is our only large water snake. When cornered, it bites aggressively, but it is not poisonous. The venomous cottonmouth is a southern snake; the northern edge of its range is Virginia.

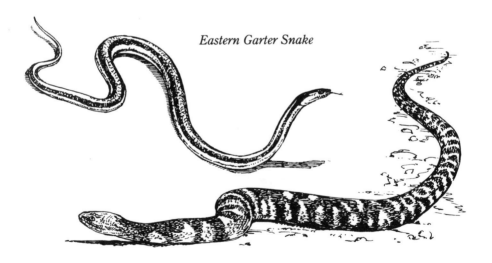

Eastern Garter Snake

Northern Water Snake

186

Amphibians

Bullfrog
Rana catesbeiana
True frog family
Length: 3"- 6"
Bullfrogs are green above; their bellies are cream or white. Their vocalization is *jug-o'-rum* with syllables slurred into a weary honk. They eat insects, other frogs, minnows, small birds, and young snakes. Note that the ridge that begins beneath their eyes curves around the ear-spot, to end above the foreleg. In the green frog, this ridge extends along the side of the back.

Breeding and egg laying take place in June or July, beneath shrubs along the shoreline. Between 12,000 and 20,000 eggs are laid in a floating film of jelly. These hatch in about a week; the tadpoles spend two or three winters under the ice before metamorphosing into miniature bullfrogs. Bullfrogs hibernate in mud from mid-October to April.

Bullfrog

Green Frog

Green Frog
Rana clamitans
True frog family
Length: 2"- 4"
Green frogs may be green, brown, or even blue above. They are whitish below. They are distinguished from bullfrogs by the ridge that begins near their eyes and extends to their rear legs. The voice is an unemphatic *tchoo*, often compared to plucking a loose banjo string. Green frogs eat insects and many other small animals.

Breeding and egg laying peak in mid-May, but continue into early summer. Floating masses of 3,500 to 5,000 eggs are attached to submerged twigs. The eggs hatch in three to six days. Tadpoles are herbivorous. They mature into frogs after one or two winters.

Leopard Frog

Pickerel Frog

Pickerel Frog
Rana palustris
True frog family
Length: 2″- 4″

Pickerel frogs are tan with dark rectangular spots. They have prominent dorsolateral ridges. Their vocalization is a steady low croak, like a nail drawn quickly along a plastic comb. Their diet consists of insects and spiders.

In the springtime females lay several thousand eggs in globular masses. Eggs hatch in two or three weeks; tadpoles become frogs after three months.

Leopard Frog
Rana pipiens
True frog family
Length: 2″- 4″

Leopard frogs are green or brown with dark round spots. They may be distinguished from pickerel frogs by the shape of the spots, and by the leopard frog's comparatively light dorsolateral ridges. The vocalization is a low snore, like two balloons being rubbed together, with occasional clucks. They eat insects and spiders.

Eggs are laid in shallow water in early to mid-spring. The tadpoles transform in July or August.

OTHER AMPHIBIANS not pictured but common in or along the Concord, Sudbury, and Assabet include the spring peeper, wood frog, and red-spotted newt.

Crustaceans

Crayfish
Cambarus species
Crayfish family
Length: 1"- 4"
Crayfish live in shallow water, seldom venturing into depths greater than five feet. They are predominantly scavengers. They eat a little of everything, but are seldom predaceous except in the confines of an aquarium, where they are terrors. Crayfish are most active at night. While feeding, they walk slowly forward, backward, or sideways. When threatened, they dart backward by doubling their fan-shaped tails and abdomens.

Females carry eggs under their abdomens between March and June; in this condition they are said to be "in berry." The young look like tiny adults. Crayfish are eaten by fish, herons, frogs, turtles, otters, mink, and raccoons.

Like other invertebrates, crayfish play a vital role in the food chain. They feed on living and dead plant and animal material, thus recycling proteins and minerals through the birds, fish, and mammals that regularly dine on them. In the absence of invertebrates, more of these nutrients, such as calcium, would wash out of freshwater communities.

Insects

Dragonflies and Damselflies

Students of insect life refer to dragonflies and damselflies by the name of their order: *Odonata*.

Dragonflies and damselflies are often seen in flight during mating. Their coupled bodies assume a puzzling configuration that bears explanation. The male's penis is on the second segment of his abdomen. Before mating the male bends the tip of his abdomen forward and transfers sperm into the penis. Then the male uses special appendages at the end of his abdomen to grasp the female by her neck. (Dragonflies grasp the back of the head; damselflies the front of the thorax.) The female then bends her abdomen forward to receive sperm from the male. The two remain attached for some time, with the female's body arched beneath that of the male.

After mating, eggs are scattered over the surface of the water (or sometimes over a smooth artificial surface that has been mistaken for water) or placed on vegetation below the surface. Different species lay eggs in different aquatic habitats such as bogs, rapids, or slow streams. The eggs of stream-dwellers are covered with a substance that becomes sticky in water, so that the eggs adhere to rocks or plants.

Odonata have "bifocals." The upper parts of their eyes are focussed to see relatively distant objects; the lower facets are for close-up vision. Damselflies and dragonflies are predators; they usually capture flying insects from below. Their legs are placed far forward, and have spines positioned to form a basket for netting insects in mid-air.

Damselflies

The wings of damselflies are held over their backs when at rest. Their eyes project from sides of the head, rather than spreading over it as do the eyes of dragonflies. Compared with their larger, stronger cousins, damselflies are more fluttering and uncertain in flight.

Damselflies overwinter as nymphs (see page 194, " Damselfly Nymphs"). After emerging, adults begin to feed on small insects such as mosquitoes. When they are ready to mate, males select territories at the sides of shady streams such as the upper Sudbury and Assabet. Eggs are deposited on or within plant stems just under the water's surface.

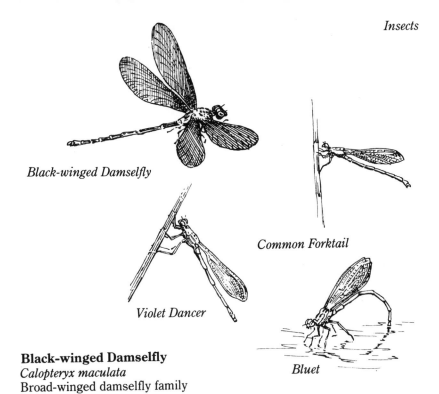

Black-winged Damselfly

Common Forktail

Violet Dancer

Bluet

Black-winged Damselfly
Calopteryx maculata
Broad-winged damselfly family
Length: 1⅝"- 1¾"
The male is metallic green with black wings. The female is dark brown, her wings smoky with a white spot.

Violet Dancer (violet tail)
Argia fumipennis violacea
Narrow-winged damselfly family
Length: 1¼"
The violet dancer male's head is black, his thorax and abdomen violet. The female is dark brown or black. The wings are clear.

Bluet
Enallagma exulans
Narrow-winged damselfly family
Length: 1¼"
The body is black with blue spots and the wings are clear. There are many similar species in the bluet genus.

Common Forktail
Ischnura verticalis
Narrow-winged damselfly family
Length: 1¼"
The male is green in front with a blue tip to the tail. The female's body is either orange in front and black behind, or blue-gray. This species is Massachusetts' most common damselfly.

Dragonflies

Dragonflies spread their wings when at rest. The leading edges of the wings are thickened so that the rest of the surface flexes when the wings are vibrated up and down. This causes forward thrust. Unlike most other four-winged insects, dragonflies' front wings rise as the hind wings beat downward. There are up to 1,600 beats per minute. The wing muscles account for a quarter of a dragonfly's weight. The result is a powerful airborne predator capable of speeds up to twenty miles an hour.

Sometimes there are "migration years," in which particularly large numbers of dragonflies appear. These may follow floods that allow larvae to spread to floodplains and mature with much less predation by fish.

Dragonflies fall to storms, kingbirds, and kestrels. Swifts and swallows take the smaller species. Frogs eat them, as do fish, which leap to catch dragonflies as they lay their eggs. Autumn frosts make an end for the rest.

Green Darner
Anax junius
Darner family
Length: 2¾"- 3⅛"
The green darner's thorax is green, the abdomen blue to grayish purple. The wings are clear with yellowish blotches. Females insert one egg into a slit cut in the stem of a submerged plant. One of the fastest and biggest of the common dragonflies, green darners are migratory.

Sympetrum
Sympetrum internum and other species
Skimmer family
Length: 1⅝"-1¾"
Males are brilliant red. Females are golden or brown.
Sympetrum are abundant from mid-summer through fall.

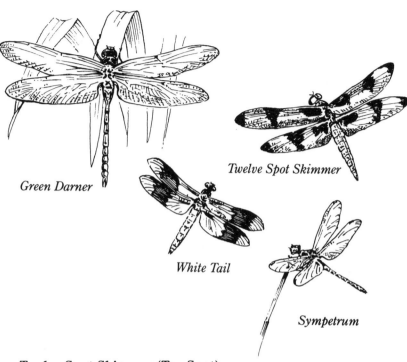

Green Darner

Twelve Spot Skimmer

White Tail

Sympetrum

Twelve Spot Skimmer (Ten Spot)
Libellula pulchella
Skimmer family
Length: 1¾″- 2¼″
The head and thorax of the twelve-spot skimmer are brown, the abdomen tan or whitish. Each wing has three brown spots. The male's wing is white between spots; the female's wing is clear between spots.

Skimmers often rest on lily pads or plants overhanging the water.

White Tail
Plathemis lydia
Skimmer family
Length: 1⅝″- 1⅞″
The male's abdomen is bright white; the female's is narrower, and brown with yellow spots. The male's wings have a broad dark band; the female resembles the female twelve-spot.

Aquatic Insect Nymphs

Dragonfly Nymphs (naiads)
Dragonflies spend one to four years as completely aquatic nymphs. They go through as many as ten molts before metamorphosing into adults. The nymphs exchange gases (carbon dioxide for oxygen) by taking in water through the tips of their abdomens. By quickly expelling this water, they can move by jet propulsion. Gills are inside the body at the lower end of abdomen.

Dragonfly nymphs prey on other insects and tiny fish. Their lower lip is long and hinged near its base so that it extends like a human arm. It is half as long as the nymph's body. At its tip are sharp claws that seize prey. Most of this remarkable structure folds under the body, while the claws rest like a mask over the lower portion of the face.

Damselfly Nymphs
Damselfly nymphs spend one winter in ponds and slow-moving streams before emerging as adults. They breathe through three feather-like gills on the tips of their abdomens, which they also wave to move themselves forward. They prey on aquatic animals using a hinged lip like that of dragonfly nymphs. They are themselves taken by trout and other fish.

Damselfly nymphs molt repeatedly before reaching maturity. From one molt to the next they become a bit more like adults; their antennae gain new joints, and wing pads appear on their thoraxes.

When ready to emerge, a nymph creeps from the water, usually in early morning. Head upward, the nymph takes a firm grasp of a plant stem. The thorax expands, tearing open the nymphal skin, from which crawls the adult. Its wings are crumpled and, for the moment, useless. They gradually expand as blood is pumped into their veins. The wings may need to harden for five hours before they are ready for flight. At the same time, the body colors intensify.

Stonefly Nymphs
Stonefly nymphs require two or three years in oxygen-rich water to develop into adults. They are tan or brown. There are about 1,500 species in this order, most of which feed on algae and plant debris. Stonefly nymphs are seldom found where the water is polluted, sharply reducing food for fish in those areas. The nymph stage of a stonefly's life lasts one to three years. To survive in an aquarium, stonefly nymphs need an oxygenating device.

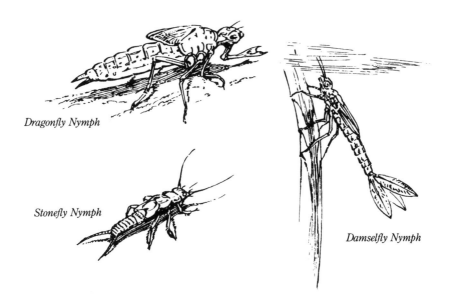

Dragonfly Nymph

Stonefly Nymph

Damselfly Nymph

Other Aquatic Insects

Backswimmers
Notonecta undulata and other species
Backswimmer family
Length: ⅜″- ½″

The forewings of backswimmers are ivory with red markings. Their undersides and legs are dark. Most aquatic animals are lighter beneath than above, to reduce their visibility under water, where all light comes from above. Backswimmers are really not exceptions to the rule; by swimming on their backs they conform to the usual pattern. Their hind legs are flattened and fringed with hair for rowing. They prey on tadpoles, insects trapped in the surface film, and even small fishes. They carry atmospheric air below with them, in troughs along their sides, and under their wings. Backswimmers can bite severely if handled. Their elongated white eggs are attached to plant stems underwater.

Water Boatmen
Corixa and other genera
Water boatman family
Length: ¼″- ½″

Water boatmen are similar in structure to backswimmers, but
they swim right side up, and they are less aggressive in their
feeding habits. They feed on microscopic animals, mosquito and
midge larvae, plant debris from the bottom, and algae, which
attracts them to birdbaths. Water boatmen trap air on their
bodies, where it glistens like silver. They are eaten in large
numbers by fish. Theirs is the largest family of freshwater bugs,
with more than two hundred species found throughout the
world.

Males call by rubbing their front legs against their heads. Water
boatmen eggs are attached to aquatic plants.

Giant Water Bugs
Belostoma species
Giant water bug family
Length: 1¼″- 1⅜″

In the genus *Belostoma*, eggs are cemented to the male's back
until they hatch, which takes about a week. This affords protection and oxygenation to the eggs. The giant water bug's hind
legs are flattened and fringed for swimming. The front legs are
for capturing prey. Giant water bugs hang head downwards in
vegetation, ready to grab small animals that come within reach
of their front legs. Once captured, a fluid is injected into the victim through the bug's beak. This fluid partially digests the
tissues of the victim, so that they may be drawn back through
the beak into the giant water bug.

The roof of the giant water bug's abdomen is concave, leaving
space between it and the wings for an air supply that can be
carried under water. Giant water bugs are powerful fliers. They
sometimes travel far from water, and are attracted to lights. A
related genus, *Lethocerus,* is sold as food in China.

When brought to the surface in a dip net, giant water bugs
sometimes play possum. Their bite is said to be very painful.

Water Striders
Gerris remigis
Water strider family
Length: ½"- ⅝"

Water striders are dark brown bugs that feed on aquatic insects. They travel on the surface film of water on four of their legs; the other pair is shorter and drawn up beneath the head, ready to capture and hold prey. Water striders move slowly by rowing their middle legs. They pounce on prey by jumping with both pairs of hind legs. Potential meals are located by ripples in the surface film, detected by sensory organs in the water strider's legs. The successful hunter jabs its beak into the prey and injects a fluid than stuns the victim and digests its tissues. Water striders eat terrestrial insects that fall into the water plus aquatic forms that come too near the surface. They willingly dispose of mosquitoes swatted and cast to the water by canoeists.

Water strider males flirt by vibrating their legs in the surface film, producing ripples provocative to the females. Parallel rows of cylindrical eggs are laid on an object at the water's edge.

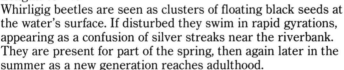

Whirligig Beetles
Dineutus and *Gyrinus* genera
Whirligig beetle family
Length: ⅜"- ⅝"

Whirligig beetles are seen as clusters of floating black seeds at the water's surface. If disturbed they swim in rapid gyrations, appearing as a confusion of silver streaks near the riverbank. They are present for part of the spring, then again later in the summer as a new generation reaches adulthood.

Adult whirligigs spend the winter in mud at the river's bottom. In the spring, eggs are deposited on submerged plants. As the eggs hatch into larvae, their parents die off. The larvae look somewhat like centipedes and live underwater, preying on mites, snails, and insects for two or three months. Then they pupate for a week, in cases of sand and debris. New adults emerge in mid- or late summer. Adults form groups during the day, but disperse to hunt the surface film for small insects at night. When alarmed they dive and cling to underwater vegetation.

Whirligig beetles' eyes are divided so that part of each eye is above the water and the other part below. The whirligig's antennae contain a receptor that detects the presence of nearby objects through compression waves in the surface film. This wonderful system of perception is not yet fully understood.

Major Routes to the Concord Basin

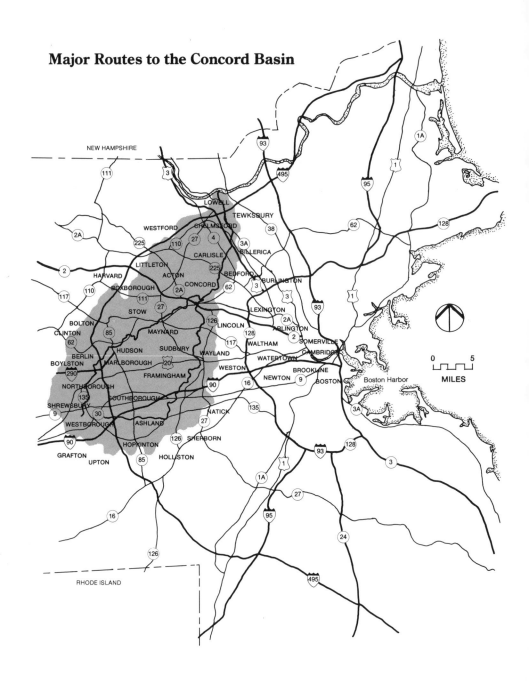

APPENDIX 1:
Suggested Outings Directory

Sudbury River

- (SU mile 0.0 - 1.7) Paddle upstream through Westborough's Cedar Swamp to the source of the Sudbury River. In this strenuous outing dense vegetation, stiff current, and tight meanders pose challenges. See "To and from Cedar Swamp Pond," page 18.

- (SU mile 2.4-3.3) This peaceful stretch of river is ideal for studying natural history, fishing, or just enjoying the intimacy of the upper Sudbury. See "Cedar Street," page 26.

- (SU mile 4.8-5.7) Another look at the upper Sudbury, on shallower water than in the previous suggestion. Some sections may require wading. See "Cordaville Road," page 26.

- (SU mile 10.3-14.6) Cruise downriver through Framingham. It is instructive and pleasing to see this populous town from the perspective of its river. See "Across Framingham," page 33.

- (SU mile 13.1-13.7) Picnic at Framingham's Simpson Drive Conservation Area. This is a logical outing for a family with young children. See "Picnic," page 33.

- (SU mile 15.4-16.1) Enjoy Framingham's prettiest stretch of the Sudbury. The oxbow/Pod Meadow area offers excellent birding. See "From Little Farms Road," page 33.

- (SU mile 16.1-18.1) The river segment between Little Farms Road and Heard Pond makes a fine flatwater natural history trip. Moderate or high water is required to navigate the channel between Heard Pond and the river. See "To Heard Pond," page 40.

- (SU mile 16.1-24.0) The heart of the Sudbury River has something for everyone. Start early and poke along all day, or use the Route 20 access point to divide the trip into two half days. See "Downstream Run," page 40.

- (SU mile 26.6-27.5) Fairhaven Bay has notable fishing. If the day is not windy, this is a good outing for beginners. See "Visit Fairhaven Bay," page 48.

- (SU mile 24.0-31.2) The lower Sudbury features wildlife habitat and fishing. At the end of this outing, the Sudbury meets the Assabet to become the Concord River. See "Downstream Run," page 48.

Assabet River

- (AS mile 0) Canoe the perimeter of the Assabet Reservoir, source of the Assabet River, a shallow impoundment rich in wildflowers, birds, and fish. See "Tour of reservoir," page 52.

- (AS mile 0) Visit a nest colony of great blue herons. See "To and from. . . ," page 52.

- (AS mile 1.0-2.6) Explore the uppermost Assabet. See "Davis Street. . .upstream," page 58.

- (AS mile 2.6-5.3) Follow the Assabet from Westborough to downtown Northborough. See "Davis Street. . .to Route 20," page 58.

- (AS mile 6.6-7.6) Still narrow and brook-like, the Assabet meanders through broad, handsome fields. See "From Boundary Street," page 66.

- (AS mile 12.2-13.6) Slowed by a dam in Hudson, the river winds through Riverside Park. This is a good trip for beginners. Canoes may be rented at the point of access. See "Hudson's Washington Street Dam," page 66.

- (AS mile 8.0-13.6) A pretty perspective on Marlborough, Berlin, and Hudson may be gained from this outing. See "Downstream from Tyler Dam," page 66.

- (AS mile 15.6-17.4) The Assabet winds around three sides of Orchard Hill, which offers a fine vista as well as unique wildlife habitat. This trip is highly recommended, but the upstream current may challenge beginners. See "From Cox Street," page 74.

- (AS mile 17.5-22.7) The marshes along this stretch offer a particularly rich variety of streamside plants. See "From Gleasondale," page 74.

- (AS mile 28.5-31.8) Paddle up the shady mouth of the Assabet. See "Upstream and back, from Old Calf Pasture," page 82.

Concord River

- (CO mile 0.1-4.5) The most historic part of this river is also the most picturesque. The gentle, unobstructed Concord is suitable for beginners. See page 88.

- (CO mile 4.5-9.5) This stretch is a popular and productive largemouth bass fishery. See "Downstream," page 94.

- (CO mile 6.6) In season, canoes may be rented at the access point for round-trip paddling in either direction.

- (CO mile 10.0-11.0) Visit the Fordway Bar and the inter section with the route of the Middlesex Canal. See "From Talbot Mill," page 99.

- (CO mile 9.5-13.3) This lowest navigable portion of the Concord is broad, flat water. See "Downstream run," page 99.

APPENDIX 2:
Canoe Training and Equipment Suppliers

Canoe training is available from:

- Appalachian Mountain Club, 5 Joy Street, Boston, MA 02108 (617) 523-0636

Canoe training and equipment are available from:

- Charles River Canoe & Kayak Center, 2401 Commonwealth Avenue, Newton, MA 02166 (617) 965-5110

Canoes and accessories are available from:

- Eastern Mountain Sports, 1400 Worcester Road, Natick, MA 01760 (508) 872-7915
- Eastern Mountain Sports, 1041 Commonwealth Avenue, Brighton, MA 02135 (617) 254-4250

- Fernald's Marine, Route 1A, Newbury, MA 01951 (978) 465-0312

- Fin and Feather Sports, Route 140, Upton, MA 01568 (508) 529-3901 **(Rentals available)**

- Fishing Tackle Annex, 14 River Street, Hudson, MA 01749 (978) 568-0575 **(Rentals available.)**

- New England Backpackers, 6 East Mountain Street, Worcester, MA 01606 (508) 853-9407

- Recreational Equipment, Inc., 279 Salem Street, Reading, MA 01867 (781) 944-5103

- Roach's Sporting Goods, 1957 Massachusetts Avenue, Cam bridge, MA 02140 (617) 876-5816

- South Bridge Boat House, Inc., 496-502 Main Street, Concord, MA 01742 (978) 369-9438 **(Rentals available)**

- Bob Smith's Wilderness House, 1048 Commonwealth Avenue, Boston, MA 02134 (617) 277-5858

United States Geological Survey topographical maps available from:

- Cartographic Information Research Service, 1002-D Hasbrouck Lab, University of Massachusetts, Amherst, MA 01003

- Eastern Mountain Sports, 1400 Worcester Road, Natick, MA 01760 (508) 872-7915

- Eastern Mountain Sports, 1041 Commonwealth Avenue, Brighton, MA 02135 (617) 254-4250

- Globe Corner Bookstore, 49 Palmer Street, Cambridge, MA 02138 (617) 497-6277

- Natick Outdoor Store, 38 North Avenue, Natick, MA 01760 (508) 653-9400

- National Cartographic Information Center, U.S. Geological Survey, Reston, VA 22092

The format of the USGS topographic quadrangle maps is being changed. Each of the new maps includes two of the old 7.5 degree quadrangles and is in metric measurements. At this writing, the 7.5 degree quadrangles are still being supplied when available. It is their names that are shown with the access points in the Canoeist's guide.

7.5 Quadrangle Name	7.5 x 15 Quadrangle Name
Billerica	Billerica
Westford	Billerica
Concord	Maynard
Maynard	Maynard
Hudson	Hudson
Lowell	Lowell
Marlborough	Marlborough
Shrewsbury	Marlborough
Milford	Milford
Holliston	Medfield
Framingham	Framingham
Natick	Framingham

APPENDIX 3:
Conservation Organizations

- Appalachian Mountain Club, 5 Joy Street, Boston, MA 02108 (617) 523-0636

- Massachusetts Audubon Society, South Great Road, Lincoln, MA 01773 (781) 259-9500

- Massachusetts Archaeological Society, P.O. Box 700 Middleborough, MA 02346

- Nature Conservancy, Eastern Regional Office, 201 Devonshire Street, 5th Floor, Boston, MA 02110

- New England Wildflower Society, Garden in the Woods, Hemenway Road, Framingham, MA 01701 (508) 877-7630

- Organization for the Assabet River, Damonmill Square, Concord, MA 01742 (978) 369-3956

- SuAsCo Watershed Coalition, P.O. Box 72, Wayland, MA 01778, (978) 461-0735

- Sudbury Valley Trustees, P.O. Box 7, Wayland, MA 01778, (978) 897-5500*

- Trustees of Reservations, 527 Essex Street, Beverly, MA 01915

Sponsored this book

APPENDIX 4:
Field Guides

We live in an age of plenty for the amateur naturalist, in terms of the volume and quality of printed matter available for self education. Nearly every bookstore has a section devoted to nature that includes a selection of field guides. The list below mentions volumes and series of potential usefulness to the Concord Basin canoeist. It is far from complete, and is intended to express a range of what is available, rather than recommendations of some guides over others.

— *A Field Guide to the Birds* with text and illustrations by Roger Tory Peterson, published by Houghton Mifflin Company, 1980.
> Paintings are organized by bird families in the order established by the American Ornithologists Union. This is the flagship of the Peterson Field Guides, a series that includes every imaginable subject for a field guide.

— *The Audubon Society Field Guide to North American Wildflowers* by William A. Niering and Nancy C. Olmstead, published by Alfred A. Knopf, 1979.
> Photographs are organized by color and shape of the flowers. Also in this series are volumes on birds and many other life forms. These photographic guides complement those using paintings; there are pros and cons to each approach. Audubon series includes more detailed text than most other field guides.

— *Summer and Fall Wildflowers of New England* by Marilyn J. Dwelley, published by Down East Enterprise, Inc., 1977.
> This series includes a volume on New England's trees and shrubs, and another about spring wildflowers. Because only this region's species are portrayed, it is often easier to find what you are looking for in these books than in guides that cover a broader area.

— *Common Marsh, Underwater, and Floating-leaved Plants of the United States and Canada* by Neil Hotchkiss, published by Dover Publications, Inc., 1972.
> This is not exactly a field guide, but botanically minded canoeists will use it as such. Line drawings of plants are organized by shape. Dover Books publishes a variety of references about this kingdom.

— *A Guide to Observing Insect Lives* by Donald W. Stokes
published by Little, Brown and Company, 1983.
> The Stokes Nature Guide series makes no attempt at
> comprehensive coverage of species, but offers a lot of
> information about the life histories of selected species.

— *Birding by Ear* by Richard K. Walton and Robert W.
Lawson, published by Houghton Mifflin Company, 1989.
> This new addition to the Peterson Field Guide Series con-
> tains three audio cassette tapes and a booklet. The
> authors have grouped patterns of similar bird songs to
> create an audio equivalent of the visual field indentifica-
> tion marks used in the Peterson series.

— *The New Field Book of Freshwater Life* by Elsie B. Klots,
published by G.P. Putnam's Sons, 1966.

— *Eastern Forests* by Ann Sutton and Myron Sutton,
published by Alfred A. Knopf, 1985.
> These are examples of books that guide learners to
> habitats or communities, rather than to particular
> kinds of plants or animals.

BIBLIOGRAPHY

Ahmadjian, Vernon, *Flowering Plants of Massachusetts.* University of Massachusetts Press, 1979.

Allen, Kristina Nilson. *On the Beaten Path.* Westborough, Massachusetts: Westborough Civic Club and Westborough Historical Society, 1984.

American Red Cross. *Canoeing.* New York: Doubleday & Company, Inc., 1956.

Angier, Bradford, and Zack Taylor. *Introduction to Canoeing.* Harrisburg, Pennsylvania: Stackpole Books, 1973.

Atkinson, Brooks, Ed. *Walden and Other Writings of Henry David Thoreau.* New York: Random House, 1937.

Atkinson, Brooks, Ed. *Selected Writings of Ralph Waldo Emerson.* New York: Random House, 1940.

Behler, John L., and F. Wayne King. *The Audubon Society Field Guide to North American Reptiles and Amphibians.* New York: Alfred A. Knopf, 1979.

Bell, Pat, and David Wright. *Rocks and Minerals.* New York: Macmillan Publishing Company, 1985.

Bolles, Frank. *Land of the Lingering Snow.* Cambridge: Houghton, Mifflin, and Company, 1892.

Brown, Lauren, *Grasses.* Boston: Houghton Mifflin Company, 1979.

Bull, John, and John Farrand, Jr. *The Audubon Society Field Guide to North American Birds.* New York: Alfred A. Knopf, 1977.

Caduto, Michael J. *Pond and Brook.* Englewood Cliffs, New Jersey: Prentice Hall, 1985.

Childs, Ethel B. *History of Stow.* Stow, Massachusetts: Stow Historical Society Publishing Company, 1983.

Cobb, Boughton. *A Field Guide to Ferns.* Boston: Houghton Mifflin Company, 1956, 1963.

Conklin, Edwin P. *Middlesex County and Its People.* New York: Lewis Historical Publishing Company, Inc., 1927.

Cronon, William. *Changes in the Land.* New York: Hill and Wang, 1983.

Cvancara, Alan M. *At the Water's Edge.* New York: John Wiley & Son., Inc., 1989.

DeGraaf, R.M., and D.D.Rudis. *Amphibians and Reptiles of New England.* Amherst: University of Massachusetts Press, 1983.

Dexter, Smith O., Ed. *Concord River, Selections from the Journals of William Brewster.* Cambridge, Massachusetts: Harvard University Press, 1937.

Dwelley, Marilyn, J. *Summer & Fall Wildflowers of New England.* Camden, Maine: Down East Enterprise, Inc., 1977.

Dwelley, Marilyn J. *Trees and Shrubs of New England.* Camden, Maine: Down East Books, 1980.

Eaton, Richard Jefferson. *A Flora of Concord.* Cambridge, Massachusetts: Museum of Comparative Zoology, Harvard University, 1974.

Epple, Anne Orth. *The Amphibians of New England.* Camden, Maine: Down East Books, 1983.

Fassett, Norman. *A Manual of Aquatic Plants.* Madison: University of Wisconsin Press, 1957.

Gilman, William H., Ed. *Selected Writings of Ralph Waldo Emerson.* New York: New American Library, 1965.

Godin, A. J. *Wild Mammals of New England.* Baltimore and London: John Hopkins University, 1977.

Griscom, Ludlow. *The Birds of Concord.* Cambridge: Harvard University Press, 1949.

Gutteridge, William H. *A Brief History of the Town of Maynard.* Maynard, Massachusetts: Town of Maynard, 1921.

Hansen, Wallace R. *Geology and Mineral Resources of the Hudson and Maynard Quadrangles.* Washington, DC: Geological Survey Bulletin 1038, 1956.

Harding, Walter, Ed., *Selections from the Journals of Henry David Thoreau.* Salt Lake City, Utah: Gibbs M. Smith, Inc., 1982.

Hauptman, Cliff. *While You Wait.* Washington, DC: Stone Wall Press, Inc. 1984.

Hauptman, Cliff. "Concord River." *Fishing Lines,* July 1989. Acton, Massachusetts: Cliff Hauptman Communications.

Hotchkiss, Neil. *Common Marsh, Underwater, & Floating-leaved Plants.* New York: Dover Publications, Inc., 1972.

Hutchins, Ross E. *Insects.* Englewood Cliffs, New Jersey: Prentice Hall, 1966.

Ingulsrud, Faith, and Bruce J. Stedman. *The Assabet Riverway Plan.* Boston, Massachusetts: Massachusetts Department of Fisheries, Wildlife, and Environmental Law Enforcement. 1986.

Jacobson, Cliff. *The Basic Essentials of Canoeing.* Merrillville, Indiana: ICS Books, Inc., 1988.

Jorgensen, Neil. *A Guide to New England's Landscape.* Chester, Connecticut: The Globe Pequot Press, 1977.

Jorgensen, Neil. *A Sierra Club Naturalist's Guide to Southern New England.* San Francisco: Sierra Club Books. 1978.

Klots, Elsie B. *The New Field Book of Freshwater Life.* New York: G.P. Putnam's Sons, 1966.

Knobel, Edward. *Field Guide to the Grasses, Sedges, and Rushes of the United States.* New York: Dover Publications, Inc., 1977, 1980.

Levine, Mirium. *A Guide to Writer's Homes in New England.* Cambridge, Watertown: Apple-wood Books, 1984.

Little, Elbert L. *The Audubon Society Field Guide to North American Trees.* New York: Alfred A. Knopf, 1980.

Malo, John. *Malo's Complete Guide to Canoeing and Canoe-Camping.* Chicago: Quadrangle Books, 1969.

Maynard Historical Committee. *History of Maynard Massachusetts, 1871-1971.* Acton, Massachusetts: Beacon Publishing Co, Inc., 1971.

McPhee, John. *The Survival of the Bark Canoe.* New York: Farrar, Straus, Giroux, 1975.

Mead, Robert Douglas. *The Canoer's Bible.* New York: Doubleday, 1976, 1989.

Milne, Lorus and Margery. *The Audubon Society Field Guide to North American Insects and Spiders.* New York: Alfred A. Knopf, 1980.

Mitchell, John Hanson. *Ceremonial Time.* New York: Doubleday and Company, Inc., 1984.

Niering, William, and Nancy Olmstead. *The Audubon Society Field Guide to North American Wildflowers.* New York: Alfred A. Knopf, 1979.

Pennak, Robert. *Freshwater Invertebrates of the United States.* New York: Ronald Press Company, 1953.

Peterson, Roger. *A Field Guide to the Birds.* Boston: Houghton Mifflin Company, 1980.

Peterson, Roger Tory and James Fisher. *Wild America.* Boston: Houghton Mifflin, 1955.

Raymo, Chet and Maureen E. Raymo. *Written in Stone.* Chester, Connecticut: Globe Pequot, 1989.

Richardson, Laurence Eaton. *Concord River.* Barre, Massachusetts: Barre Publishers, 1964.

River Guide Committee. *AMC River Guide, Massachusetts, Connecticut, Rhode Island.* Boston, Massachusetts: Appalachian Mountain Club, 1985.

Riviere, Bill. *Pole, Paddle, & Portage.* New York: Van Nostrand Reinhold Company, 1969.

Russell, Howard S. *A Long, Deep Furrow.* Hanover and London: University Press of New England, 1982.

Russell, Howard S. *Indian New England Before the Mayflower.* Hanover and London: University Press of New England, 1980.

Screpetis, Arthur. "Aquatic Plants of Massachusetts." *Massachusetts Wildlife,* Volume XXXIII Number 3. Massachusetts Division of Fisheries and Wildlife.

Shuttleworth, Floyd, and Herbert Zim. *Non-Flowering Plants.* New York: Golden Press, 1967.

Simmons, William S. *Spirit of the New England Tribes.* Hanover and London: University Press of New England, 1986.

Stokes, Donald W. *Guide to Bird Behavior Volume I.* Boston and Toronto: Little, Brown, and Company, 1979.

Stokes, Donald W., *Guide to Observing Insect Lives.* Boston and Toronto: Little, Brown, and Company, 1979.

Sutton, Ann, and Myron Sutton. *Eastern Forests.* New York: Alfred A. Knopf, 1985.

Teal, Edwin Way. *The Strange Lives of Familiar Insects.* New York: Dodd, Mead and Company, 1962.

Terres, John K. *Audubon Society Encyclopedia of North American Birds.* New York: Alfred A. Knopf, 1982.

Thompson, Betty Flanders. *The Changing Face of New England.* Boston: Houghton Mifflin Company, 1958.

Thompson, Gerald, and Jennifer Coldry. *The Pond.* Cambridge, Massachusetts: MIT Press, 1984.

Thoreau, Henry D. *A Week on the Concord and Merrimack Rivers.* New York: Thomas Y. Crowell, 1911.

Ursin, Michael J. *Life in and Around Freshwater Wetlands.* New York: Thomas Y. Crowell Company, 1975.

Walton, Richard K. *Birds of the Sudbury River Valley — An Historical Perspective.* Lincoln, Massachusetts: Massachusetts Audubon Society, 1984.

Whitaker, Jr., John O. *The Audubon Society Field Guide to North American Mammals.* New York: Alfred A. Knopf, 1980.

Zwinger, Ann and Edwin Way Teal. *A Conscious Stillness.* New York: Harper & Row, 1982.

Acknowledgements

The precursor to this volume was the *Concord and Sudbury Rivers User Guide and Resource Description*, produced in 1987, which was a joint undertaking of the Sudbury Valley Trustees, the U.S. National Park Service, the U.S. Fish and Wildlife Service, the Massachusetts Department of Environmental Management, the Massachusetts DEQE, now Department of Environmental Protection, and the SuAsCo Watershed Association. Special thanks is due Steven Golden, Program Manager of the National Park Service's Branch of River and Trail Conservation, and to Richard Walton who wrote its canoe narrative and assembled the resource description with the assistance of John Organ, Christopher Leahy, Richard Forster, Charles Roth, John Lindenberg, and Pete Jackson. The William P. Wharton Trust provided vital initial financial support.

The project was brought to its present form by the Sudbury Valley Trustees, under the leadership of executive director Allen Morgan. Other SVT personnel who made direct contributions were Barbara Mackey, Al Sanborn, and Charles Grant, who field-checked canoe access points.

Bill Miller provided geological information, including identification of rock samples from exposures along the rivers. Other information was provided by Bob McDonald, Gay Gibson, Dorothy and Emily Perkins, Joe Bergin, Michele Monjeau, Arthur Screpetis, Tanya Largy, and Shirley Blancke.

The manuscript benefitted from comments made by readers at many stages. My thanks to Annie Hale, David Bastille, Cecile Costine, Jed and Sally Watters, Barbara Mackey, Dick Walton, Ed Moses, Roger DeRosa, Gay Gibson, Bob McDonald, Judy Mack, Steve Morrissey, Claudia Kopkowski, Charles Grant, botanist Ray Angelo, aquatic biologist Arthur Screpetis of the Massachusetts Division of Water Pollution Control, and archaeologists Tanya Largy and Shirley Blancke. Also to: Robert O'Connor of the Metropolitan District Commission, Michele Monjeau of Massachusetts Riverways Programs, John Lindenberg and Dave Halliwell of the Massachusetts Division of

Fisheries and Wildlife, geographer George Lewis, Steve Golden of the National Park Service, Al Sanborn, Stephen Clouter, and Allen Morgan.

Pleasurable research was done by canoe, usually with the help of another canoeist. Many thanks to my companions on the water, who often did more than their share of paddling: Al Sanborn, Annie Hale, Tim Caswell, Molly McAdow, Vincent Valvo, Deborah Costine, Jon Klein, John and Pat Merritt, Hank Bennett, Allen Morgan, and Cliff Hauptman. Thanks to Peter Kallander for taking me in his plane for an aerial view of the rivers.

It has been a privilege to collaborate with illustrator Gordon Morrison.

The map on page 108 was adapted with permission from *Spirit of the New England Tribes* by William S. Simmons, University of New England Press, 1986. The excerpt from Ludlow Griscom's *Birds of Concord* that appears on page 118 is reprinted by permission of Harvard University Press.

Ron McAdow

Ron McAdow grew up in Illinois, and after graduation from the University of Chicago, he moved to Massachusetts, where he was surprised by the charms of the New England landscape. He spent six years in Holliston, making animated films for children's television. His award-winning films *Hank the Cave Peanut* and *Captain Silas* are featured in library film screenings across the nation.

In the late 1970s Ron lived in Texas for three years, working in environmental education. In the 1980s he has done a variety of writing projects, including a quarterly newsletter for Sudbury Valley Trustees called *Westborough Resources*. He directed a camp for six summers, and has taught at the Eliot Montessori School in Natick and the Charles River School in Dover.

Ron lives with his wife Deborah Costine who is a puppeteer, and their daughter Molly, on the north bank of the Sudbury River in Southborough, Massachusetts.

Gordon Morrison

Gordon Morrison is an artist and illustrator whose books include *Newcomb's Wildflower Guide, The Birdwatcher's Companion, The Curious Naturalist, A Guide to Eastern Forests,* as well as several other Peterson field guides. His illustrations have appeared in periodicals that run a broad and eclectic gamut: *Horticulture, Fortune, Ranger Rick, Playboy, Seventeen*, and the *New York Conservationist.*

Gordon is a native of Boston who studied art at The Museum School of Fine Arts and the Butera School in Boston. His murals grace high schools in Sharon and Stoughton, Massachusetts and his dioramas can be found at the Boston Zoological Society, The Public Service Company of New Hampshire, and the Massachusetts Audubon Society. Gordon's work is in art galleries and collections throughout the east coast.

He lives with his wife and three children in North Attleborough, Massachusetts.

Index

Mink, 24, 179, 184, 189
life history of, 181
Minuteman National Historic Park, 86
Morgan, Allen, xi, 118
Mosses from an Old Manse, excerpt, 49
Motorboats, 93, 94, 97
Multiflora rose, 126
Musketaquid, 13, 38, 48
Muskrat, 64, 132, 133, 137, 142, 147, 148, 181
life history of, 179
Mustela vison (mink), 24, 179, 181, 184, 189
Myosotis scorpioides (True forget-me-not), 135
Myotis lucifugus (little brown bat), 183
Myriophyllum humile (low watermilfoil), 39, 146-147
Myrtle Street Dam Access Point, 23

– N –

Nashawtuc Hill, 48, 82
Nashoba Brook, 82
Naturalists of the Concord Basin, 116-119
Nature, 86
excerpt, 116
Nerodia sipedon (northern water snake), 186
Newt, red-spotted, 188
Newton, Andrew, 25
Nichols Dam. *See* Dams, Nichols
Nichols Reservoir. *See* Assabet Reservoir
Nightshade, bittersweet, 128-129
Nipmuck. *See* Algonquian-speaking tribes
North Bridge Visitor's Center, 87
North Bridge, Old, 85-86
Northborough, 110, 113
canoeing in, 55-66
Northern oriole, 156-157
Northern pike, 11
Notonecta undulata (back-swimmers), 195
Nuphar variegatum

(yellow pond lily), 17, 109, 142-143
Nuthatch, white-breasted, 154-155
Nyanza toxic waste site, 25, 116
Nycticorax nycticorax (black-crowned night heron), 165
Nymphaea odorata (white water lily), 117, 142-143
Nymphs, damselfly, 194-195
Nymphs, dragonfly, 194-195
Nymphs, stonefly, 194-195

– O –

Oak, swamp white, 124
Oats, water. *See* Wild rice
October Farm, 118
Odocoileus virginianus (white-tailed deer) 132, 133, 148, 182
Odonata, 190-194
Old Calf Pasture Access Point, 1, 45, 48, 79, 82, 85, 88, 200
Old Middlesex Turnpike Access Point, 91-93
Old Sawmill Dam Access Point, 55, 58, 61, 63
Oleander, water. *See* Loosestrife, swamp
Ondatra zibethicus (muskrat), 64, 132, 133, 137, 142, 147, 148, 181
life history, 179
Orchard Hill, 71, 72, 74, 103, 160, 161, 200
Oriole, northern, (Baltimore), 156, 157
Osmunda cinnamomea (cinnamon fern), 141
Osmunda regalis (royal fern), 140
Osprey, 46, 170
Otter, river, 17, 24, 181
Oxbow in Sudbury River, 32, 33, 38, 199

– P –

Painted turtle, 87

Pandion haliaetus (osprey), 170
Pantry Brook, 45
Parus atricapillus (black-capped chickadee), 18, 155
Parus bicolor (tufted titmouse), 155
Pawtucket. *See* Algonquian-speaking tribes
Peabody, Sophia, 86
Pelham Island Road Access Point, 35
Peltandra virginica (arrow arum), 134
Pepperbush, sweet, 15, 127
Pepperwort. *See* Clover, water
Perca flavescens (yellow perch), 11, 47, 176-177
Perch, white, 177
Perch, yellow, 11, 47, 176-177
Phalaris arundinacea (reed canarygrass), 139
Philohela minor (American woodcock), 160-161
Pickerelweed, 73, 87, 133-134
Picoides pubescens (downy woodpecker), 154-155
Pike, northern, 11, 177
Pine, white, 64
Plathemis lydia (white tail dragonfly), 193
Pod Meadow, 32, 38, 199
Podilymbus podiceps (pied-billed grebe), 168-169
Pollution, 113-116
mercury in Sudbury River, 115
nutrient, 114
Hoccomocco Pond, 56
removed by cattails, 137
surplus nutrients, 137
from wastewater, 80
Polygonum coccineum (swamp

222